Called to Full Communion

A Study Resource for Lutheran-Anglican Relations
including The Waterloo Declaration

prepared by the Joint Working Group
of the Evangelical Lutheran Church in Canada
and the Anglican Church of Canada
December, 1997

1998
Anglican Book Centre
600 Jarvis Street
Toronto, Ontario
M4Y 2J6

Canadian Cataloguing in Publication Data

Called to full communion: a study resource for Lutheran-Anglican relations (including the Waterloo Declaration)

ISBN 1-55126-215-0

1. Anglican Church of Canada — Relations — Evangelical Lutheran Church in Canada.
2. Evangelical Lutheran Church in Canada — Relations — Anglican Church in Canada.
3. Christian union — Anglican Church of Canada.
4. Christian union — Evangelical Lutheran Church in Canada I. Joint Working Group of the Evangelical Lutheran Church in Canada and the Anglican Church of Canada.

BX5618.E92C34 1998   280'.042   C98-930261-X

TABLE OF CONTENTS

PREFACE

The Evangelical Lutheran Church in Canada and the Anglican Church of Canada have been in dialogue for a considerable period of time. Sharing together in many ways — in worship, in theological discussion, in mission — we have come to know each other more and more. In some places we have formed joint ministries, in others we have shared facilities. Nationally, the Anglican House of Bishops and the Lutheran Conference of Bishops have agreed to gather with each other once a year. Through all this, we are making the happy discovery that we belong to and are at home with one another. More than being friends, we are genuine companions in the Body of Christ.

This age has been called "the ecumenical century," and, in spite of some dark moments, there has been a remarkable growth in mutual understanding and respect among the churches. Conversation with one another has helped our hearts grow warmer and, in many areas of mission, we have been able to make common cause for the sake of the gospel. In Canada, at the end of this century and on the eve of a new millennium, the Anglican-Lutheran conversation is a concrete sign of hope. The call to full communion between our two churches can give real expression to that hope. It also has the potential to promote a deeper passion for unity in the wider Christian community.

Certainly, a realization of the goal of full communion will bring us into a profound and significant relationship. This requires prayer, good will, and clarity of thought as to our assumptions about faith and order. This study guide is offered to help us do that. In this resource you will find much to talk about, to think about and, most of all, to pray about together. We commend its use in all our churches, and especially, wherever possible, by gatherings of Anglicans and Lutherans together.

May God bless you as you make use of this resource. And may God give us all the heart of Jesus Christ whose desire for us is that we become one.

Michael G. Peers
Archbishop and Primate
The Anglican Church of
Canada

Telmor Sartison
National Bishop
Evangelical Lutheran Church in
Canada

How to Use This Book

Called to Full Communion is a resource book for Lutherans and Anglicans in Canada as our two churches get ready to make decisions in 2001 about a possible relationship of full communion.

It contains the text of the Draft Declaration, which has been approved for circulation in our churches for study, but which is still open to suggestions for improvement.

"Questions Commonly Asked" contains a series of questions that members of the Joint Working Group have been asked as people around the country study the issues. It is not a definitive commentary, but will serve as a resource for people as they read the Draft Declaration and participate in the study sessions. A commentary will be prepared for publication later in 1998.

There are two suggested outlines for study sessions, one for use in one day and one for use in four sessions. Possible uses include joint clergy days; deanery/conference gatherings; joint parish study; Lenten study programs; or as part of a larger educational event in the churches.

"Who We Are" contains some basic information about each of our churches, and "Dates of Interest" highlights some of the developments between our two communions.

A section summarizing "Key Documents" is followed by excerpts from some of these, which will permit further in-depth discussion of the issues.

A brief glossary is provided of "Some Words and Terms" used in the Draft Declaration and in our churches.

"For More Information" provides the names of and ways to contact staff and members of the Joint Working Group.

Please feel free to adapt the material in ways that suit your needs.

THE WATERLOO DECLARATION
(as approved by the Joint Working Group)

Draft
23 June 1997

*Proposed text to be considered by
the National Convention of the Evangelical Lutheran Church in
Canada and the General Synod of the Anglican Church of Canada
Waterloo, Ontario
2001*

Preface

1. In John 17:20–21, our Lord prayed that Christians might all be one so that the world might believe in Christ through the witness of our unity. The 20th century has given rise to an increase of movements which seek to give visible expression to this prayer. Christians have begun to see the fulfillment of Jesus' words as they unite in action to address the needs of local and global communities. The churches themselves have entered into partnerships at every level, from the neighbourhood to the world, through councils of churches, theological dialogues, and covenants which have fostered greater understanding in the search for common witness and visible unity. All these steps have moved us towards a healing of ancient divisions, including those which occurred during the 16th century in Europe.

2. Lutherans and Anglicans are graced in that we can respond to this prayer for unity without having experienced formal separation from one another. We share a common heritage as catholic churches of the Reformation. Despite our previous geographic, linguistic and cultural differences, in recent years we have discovered in one another a shared faith and spirituality. This discovery has called us into a search for more visible unity in mission and ministry.

3. On the international scene, the Lutheran World Federation and the Anglican Consultative Council have participated in a number of formal discussions since 1972. These conversations were encouraged by the international multilateral consensus document *Baptism, Eucharist and Ministry* (Faith and Order Paper 111, WCC, 1982). In 1987, an international Lutheran-Anglican consultation on *episcope* was held in Niagara [Falls, Ontario]. From this gathering some specific recommendations were directed to the churches for their discussion. Consideration of these recommendations led in northern Europe to *The Porvoo Common Statement* (1993), and in the United States to the *Concordat of Agreement* (1997).

4. In 1983, Canadian Lutherans and Anglicans met to discuss the implications for the churches in Canada of the ongoing dialogue between Lutherans and Episcopalians in the United States. From this meeting emerged the Canadian Lutheran-Anglican Dialogue (CLAD), whose first series of meetings led to the publication of its *Report and Recommendations* (April, 1986). This report gave impetus to the desire of the two churches to produce an agreement which could provide a basis for the sharing of the eucharist between our churches.

5. A second series of discussions (CLAD II) resulted in the agreement *Interim Sharing of the Eucharist*, which was approved in 1989 by the National Convention of the Evangelical Lutheran Church in Canada and by the General Synod of the Anglican Church of Canada. In that agreement, we

> i.   agreed to live in a relationship of interim eucharistic sharing
> ii. acknowledged one another as churches in which the Gospel is preached and taught
> iii. committed ourselves to share a common life in mission and service, to pray for and with one another, and to share resources

6. The experience of six years of interim eucharistic sharing led the two churches in 1995 to take further steps towards full communion. The National Convention and the General Synod renewed the Interim Eucharistic Sharing Agreement until 2001 and further agreed

    i. to request all neighbouring congregations to undertake joint projects and celebrate the eucharist together annually

   ii. to receive one another's lay members, when moving from one church to the other with the same status (baptized/communicant/confirmed) which they held in their first church

  iii. to foster the development and implementation of agreements which permit an ordained minister (priest or pastor) to serve the people of both churches, including presiding at the sacraments of the Church, wherever, and according to whichever rite, the local bishop of each church deems appropriate

  iv. to develop structures with the purpose of evaluating and improving the bishop's ministry through collegial and periodic review

   v. to call for our two churches to move towards full communion by 2001

7. Our two churches are using the following definition of full communion.

> Full communion is understood as a relationship between two distinct churches or communions in which each maintains its own autonomy while recognizing the catholicity and apostolicity of the other, and believing the other to hold the essentials of the Christian faith. In such a relationship, communicant members of each church would be able freely to communicate at the altar of the other, and there would be freedom of ordained ministers to officiate sacramentally in either church. Specifically, in our context, we understand this to include transferability of members; mutual recognition and interchangeability of ministries; freedom to use each other's liturgies; freedom to participate in each other's ordinations and installations of clergy, including bishops; and structures for consultation to express, strengthen, and enable our common life, witness, and service, to the glory of God and the salvation of the world.

8. In a spirit of thanksgiving for what God has already accomplished in us, and with confidence and hope for what God has prepared for

the whole Church, we believe we can now act in visible witness to the unity which is ours in Jesus Christ. We are taking the next step in our common pilgrimage of faith in the belief that it will be of service to a greater unity.

Proposed Joint Declaration

We, the Evangelical Lutheran Church in Canada and the Anglican Church of Canada, make the following acknowledgements and commitments:

A. Acknowledgements

1. We declare that in each church "the Gospel is preached in its purity and the holy sacraments are administered according to the Gospel" (Augsburg Confession VII), that in each church "the pure Word of God is preached, and the Sacraments ... duly ministered according to Christ's ordinance in all those things that of necessity are requisite to the same." (Article XIX of *The Thirty-Nine Articles*)

2. We acknowledge that both our churches share in the common confession of the apostolic faith. (*Report and Recommendations, CLAD I, 1986*)

3. We acknowledge that personal, collegial and communal oversight (episcope) is embodied and exercised in both churches in a variety of forms, in continuity of apostolic life, mission and ministry. (*The Porvoo Common Statement, 1993*)

4. We acknowledge that the episcopal office is valued and maintained in both our churches as a visible sign expressing and serving the Church's unity and continuity in apostolic life, mission and ministry. (*The Porvoo Common Statement, 1993*)

5. We acknowledge that one another's ordained ministries are given by God as instruments of divine grace and as possessing not only the inward call of the Spirit, but also Christ's commission through his body, the Church (An Appeal to all Christian People, Lambeth Conference, 1920); and that these ministries are the gifts of God's Spirit to equip the people of God for the work of ministry (Ephesians 4:11–12).

6. In the light of the above agreements, we make the following statements:

a.   The Anglican Church of Canada hereby recognizes the full authenticity of the ordained ministries presently existing within the Evangelical Lutheran Church in Canada, acknowledging its pastors as priests in the Church of God and its bishops as chief pastors exercising a ministry of *episcope* over the jurisdictional areas of the Evangelical Lutheran Church in Canada in which they preside.

b.   The Evangelical Lutheran Church in Canada hereby recognizes the full authenticity of the ordained ministries of bishops, priests, and deacons presently existing within the Anglican Church of Canada, acknowledging its priests as pastors in the Church of God and its bishops as chief pastors exercising a ministry of *episcope* over the jurisdictional areas of the Anglican Church of Canada in which they preside.

c.   The Anglican Church of Canada and the Evangelical Lutheran Church in Canada each understands the bishops of both churches to be ordained for life service of the Gospel in the pastoral ministry of the historic episcopate, although tenure in office may be terminated by retirement, resignation or conclusion of term, subject to the constitutional provisions of the respective churches.

B. Declaration of Full Communion

We declare the Evangelical Lutheran Church in Canada and the Anglican Church of Canada to be in full communion.

C. Commitments

As churches in full communion, we now commit ourselves:

1. to welcome persons ordained in either of our churches to the office of bishop, priest/pastor or deacon to serve, by invitation and in accordance with any regulations which may from time to time be in force, in that ministry in the receiving church without re-ordination;

2. regularly to invite one another's bishops to participate in the laying on of hands at the ordination of bishops as a sign of the unity and continuity of the Church, and to invite pastors and priests to participate in the laying on of hands at the ordination of pastors or priests in each other's churches;

3. to work towards a common understanding of diaconal ministry;

4. to establish appropriate forms of collegial and conciliar consultation on significant matters of faith and order, mission and service;

5. to encourage regular consultation and collaboration among members of our churches at all levels, to promote the formulation and adoption of covenants for common work in mission and ministry, and to facilitate learning and exchange of ideas and information on theological, pastoral, and mission matters;

6. to establish a Joint Commission to nurture our growth in communion, to coordinate the implementation of this Declaration, and report to the decision-making bodies of both our churches;

7. to hold joint meetings of national, regional and local decision-making bodies wherever practicable, and

8. to continue to work together for the full visible unity of the whole Church of God.

Conclusion

We rejoice in our Declaration as an expression of the visible unity of our churches in the one Body of Christ. We are ready to be co-workers with God in whatever tasks of mission serve the Gospel. We give glory to God for the gift of unity already ours in Christ, and we pray for the fuller realization of this gift in the entire Church.

(to be signed, if approved, by the National Bishop of the Evangelical Lutheran Church in Canada and the Primate of the Anglican Church of Canada)

Notes

Wording in sections A.2, 3, 4, 5; and C.1, 2, 3, 4, 5 is derived from *The Porvoo Common Statement* © David Tustin and Tore Furberg. Published in 1993 by Church House Publishing for the Council for Christian Unity of the General Synod of the Church of England.

Wording in section A.6 is derived from *Concordat of Agreement* between the Episcopal Church and the Evangelical Lutheran Church in America, revised January, 1997, published for study by the Office of Ecumenical Relations of the Episcopal Church.

Questions Commonly Asked about the Proposals for Full Communion

*between the Anglican Church of Canada and the
Evangelical Lutheran Church in Canada*

1. Why a relationship between these particular churches?

Anglicans and Lutherans share a common heritage:

- as part of the church of the West before the Reformation
- as churches shaped by the Reformation itself
- as established national state churches in Europe
- as churches that have a national expression in Canada while being part of worldwide communions

Both churches engaged in and emerged from the Reformation believing themselves to be part of the one, holy, catholic, and apostolic church. They believed themselves to hold the same faith, to preach the same Word, to celebrate the same sacraments, and to exercise the same ministry, as the apostles, and to be in continuity with them and with the church throughout the ages.

Fifteen years of dialogue in this country, and far more internationally, have convinced both churches that the other is a church in which the Word is truly preached and taught and that each possesses a ministry of Word and Sacrament that is fruitful in terms of faith and salvation for its members. On fundamentals of doctrine, the two communions agree.

For many years in Canada, Lutherans were not much known to the dominant culture because of language barriers. As recent generations have come to speak English predominantly, Lutherans have played a more visible role in the religious life of Canada. In social justice coalitions, in councils of churches and ministerials, in neighbourhood outreach and social events, Anglicans and Lutherans have met each other, and often find themselves on common ground.

Internationally, Anglican-Lutheran dialogue activity increased dramatically in the 1980s, spurred on in part by the invitation issued by *Baptism, Eucharist and Ministry*. The conversation among Lutherans, and the move to adopt the episcopacy in a number of Lutheran churches that had not previously had bishops (at least by that title), made it more possible for Anglicans to recognize themselves in their Lutheran counterparts.

2. Anglicans wonder, "Which Lutherans are we talking about?"

The Evangelical Lutheran Church in Canada, the largest Lutheran body in Canada, was formed in 1986 by a merger of the Lutheran Church in America (Canada Section) and the Evangelical Lutheran Church of Canada. The ELCIC is a member church of the Lutheran World Federation. Other Lutheran church bodies, namely Lutheran Church — Canada (Missouri Synod), Wisconsin Synod, Lutheran Brethren, and others, are not part of the conversations.

Related to the ELCIC are congregations that retain a close association with the European Lutheran churches from which their members came, including the churches of Latvia, Lithuania, Estonia, and Finland; their pastors are also pastors of the ELCIC. The Church of England recognized the parent churches as being in communion with Canterbury just before World War II, and Canada concurred. Thus the Anglican Church of Canada already recognizes some Lutheran pastors, and has participated in the consecration of the bishop of the Latvian church abroad.

3. What is actually being proposed?

The Joint Working Group was given a mandate by the national meetings of 1995 to address outstanding issues such as the meaning of "full authenticity of ministries," the distinctions of the three-fold ministry, and the mutual participation of the bishops of each church in the installation/consecration of bishops.

The result of their work is the Draft Declaration, which outlines the proposals for full communion between the two churches. It is explained in the questions and answers that follow. There will also be a commentary on the Draft Declaration available later in 1998.

4. What is full communion?

The Draft Declaration uses the following definition, which was developed by the Canadian Lutheran-Anglican Dialogue (CLAD II).

> Full communion is understood as a relationship between two distinct churches or communions in which each maintains its own autonomy while recognizing the catholicity and apostolicity of the other, and believing the other to hold the essentials of the Christian faith. In such a relationship, communicant members of each church would be able freely to communicate at the altar of the other, and there would be freedom of ordained ministers to officiate sacramentally in either church.   Specifically, in our context, we understand this to include transferability of members; mutual recognition and interchangeability of ministries; freedom to use each other's liturgies; freedom to participate in each other's ordinations and installations of clergy, including bishops; and structures for consultation to express, strengthen, and enable our common life, witness, and service, to the glory of God and the salvation of the world.

5. But will this be a merger, like the organic union proposed between the Anglican Church of Canada and the United Church that was rejected in 1975, or like the merger that created the ELCIC?

No. The ELCIC was a merger of two Lutheran bodies. Full communion will be a relationship of sister churches, such as the Anglican Church of Canada already has with the Philippine Independent Church, the Mar Thoma Church, and the churches of the Bonn Agreement (old Catholic churches in communion with the Archbishop of Utrecht). While there will be structures for mutual consultation, each church will retain its autonomy. The ELCIC does not presently have a full communion relationship with any non-Lutheran church body.

6.   Does this mean that the churches will have full visible unity?

This relationship would be one step, between two churches, on the way to full visible unity. The full visible unity of the church throughout the world remains the final vision and goal of the ecumenical movement. Both churches continue to be committed to working towards building that communion with all partners in the ecumenical movement.

7. How much of the definition of full communion have we already achieved in Canada?

Over the last 15 years, Canadian Anglicans and Lutherans have taken many steps together.

a. agreement in faith

The Interim Sharing of the Eucharist Agreement of 1989 was based on an acknowledgment that we each believe the other to be churches that agree on the essentials of the Christian faith. It stated that each recognizes the other as a church in which the gospel is preached and taught (cf. *CLAD I, Report and Recommendations*).

b. transferability of membership

Both churches believe that membership in the church is conferred by baptism. We recognize each other's baptism. In practice, active adult membership, such as entitles one to voting privileges, was often linked to confirmation. In 1995, both churches agreed that confirmation would not be required of anyone moving from one communion to the other, but that members would "be received with the same status (baptized/communicant/confirmed) that they held in the ELCIC or ACC. A service of reception is appropriate to mark such an event.

The Council of General Synod of the Anglican Church of Canada approved the following resolution in May, 1997 as a way of implementing this resolution:

Lay people of the Evangelical Lutheran Church in Canada moving to the Anglican Church of Canada are to be received with the same status (baptized/communicant/confirmed) which they held in the ELCIC. The intention is to have Lutherans received into an Anglican congregation by a process of welcoming new members. Lutheran pastors would be asked to write a letter of transfer on behalf of a Lutheran who is transferring to an Anglican congregation. The rubrical directions for welcoming new members from *Occasional Celebrations* would be appropriate. The rite of reception, including laying on of hands (as on pages 106–107 of the *Canadian Book of Occasional Offices* (1964) or page 161 of the *Book of Alternative Services*) would also be appropriate if requested by the individual. Confirmation by episcopal laying on of hands is not normally appropriate for those who have been confirmed, but may be done at the request of the individual.

Those so transferred would be eligible for voting in church meetings, serving on church bodies, attending synods, etc. subject to operative standards regarding age and communicant status.

The ELCIC has a practice of "transferring membership" when an adult voting member goes to another congregation, whereby their "being in good standing" is communicated to the new congregation. The Joint Working Group has proposed to the National Church Council changes to the *Model Constitution for Congregations* in the ELCIC, which will permit someone to transfer their membership from an Anglican congregation to a Lutheran congregation with the same status that they held in their own.

It is appropriate for those moving to a congregation in the other church to receive instruction in the structure and governance of the receiving church. (Such books as *This Evangelical Lutheran Church of Ours* and *This Anglican Church of Ours* or *This Is Our Faith* would be helpful.)

It is possible for members to transfer back again.

c. mutual recognition and interchangeability of ministries

At the moment, Lutheran pastors may serve Anglican congregations and vice versa, in particular circumstances, and according to specific terms agreed to by both bishops. It is recognized that in certain areas, whether due to geography, language, availability, or pastoral necessity, ministry can be best provided by a cleric of the other church. At the moment, the ministries are not, strictly speaking, "interchangeable"; the clergy function as licensed/rostered clergy of their own church, "on loan" to the other church.

The Draft Declaration intends to declare the full recognition of ordained ministries in each other's churches. This would make it possible for all priests and pastors to serve in both churches, subject to licensing and rostering agreements (cf. Draft Declaration Acknowledgments 6.).

d. freedom to use each other's liturgies

As of 1995, in particular circumstances, and with the agreement of both bishops, a minister of one church can function in the other using whichever rite the bishops agree is appropriate. Because of the growth in liturgical agreement, there is a great deal of similarity between our common liturgical forms, especially between the *Book of Alternative Services* and the *Lutheran Book of Worship*.

If ministries are mutually recognized, there could be full interchangeable use of liturgies, subject to the approval of the bishops concerned.

e. freedom to participate in each other's ordinations and installations of clergy, including bishops

When full communion is established, each church would be free to participate in each other's ordinations/installations, not as intending to supply something missing in the other, but as a sign of our common mission and ministry (cf. Declaration C.2.).

f. structures for consultation to express, strengthen and enable our common life, witness, and service, to the glory of God and the salvation of the world

It is one thing to agree that we are sister churches, and another to act like it. Our two churches will be seeking to find every way they can to work together in Christ's service. The Canadian Lutheran-Anglican Dialogue was concluded and a Joint Working Group was established precisely to provide a place for making common proposals, for exchanging information about important issues in each of our churches and trying to seek a common will, and for engaging in common action of mission and service. This is the first step of greater structural collaboration. The Draft Declaration outlines specific ways in which the two churches will be able to work, speak, and act together in common witness.

The commitment of bishops of both churches to meet together annually is one expression of our intention to consult each other more closely and deliberately. The churches are being asked to consider inviting representatives to participate in each other's national councils, and even to have a concurrent meeting of the councils. The concurrent meetings in 2001 of the General Synod (of the Anglican Church of Canada) and the National Convention (of the Evangelical Lutheran Church in Canada) would be another such expression.

8. How does the Draft Declaration uphold the priesthood of all believers?

This belief is part of the faith shared between our two churches, identified by the earlier theological dialogue. The Draft Declaration focuses on ordained ministry because this is the area where there are points of divergence in practice. It begins, however, by acknowledging the ministry of the whole church, exercised by all its members. Both our churches agree that ministry, including priestly and episcopal ministry, is a gift from Christ to the whole church. When our churches ordain individuals they place the person ordained in a particular ministry within the priesthood of all believers (*CLAD I, Statement on Ordained Ministry*, pp. 86–87).

9. Lutherans wonder, "Would we be giving up part of our heritage?"

Lutherans would retain their confessional heritage, including the confessional writings and the central doctrine of justification by grace through faith. In the new relationship of full communion, Lutherans will build upon and expand this heritage as a Church of the Reformation. In so doing, they would honour their own history, as well as affirm the insights and recommendations of *The Niagara Report* and the *Baptism, Eucharist and Ministry* document.

10. Anglicans wonder, "Would we be giving up part of our heritage?"

Being an ecumenical church is part of the Anglican heritage. A three-fold ministry of bishops, priests, and deacons is also part of that heritage. Anglicans would not be changing their own self-understanding, but recognizing that another church, which for historic reasons has reached different conclusions without in any way abandoning its sense of continuity with the apostolic church, is indeed a church in the tradition of the apostles. By the act of entering full communion, we would each come to share a larger heritage.

11. Anglicans wonder, "What about the historic episcopate?"

Anglicans over the centuries have had a variety of ways of explaining the relationship of the role of the bishop to the apostolicity and faithfulness of the church. One of the four points considered essential for forming a basis for negotiation with any other Christian bodies with a view to union in the 1888 Lambeth Quadrilateral was: "The Historic Episcopate, locally adapted in the methods of its administration to the varying needs of the nations and peoples called of God into the Unity of His Church" (cf. *The Lambeth Quadrilateral*, p. 80).

Since we agreed on the other points of the Lambeth Quadrilateral (scriptures, creeds, and sacraments), the dialogue spent much of its energy in coming to understand how our two churches have adapted the episcopate. In that respect, the historic episcopate has certainly formed the basis for negotiation between our two churches.

It was because of particular historical circumstances, and not for theological reasons, that some Lutheran churches did not have bishops ordained in exact continuity by the laying on of hands by other bishops. Lutherans in Canada, while not viewing the historic episcopate as a necessity, are now prepared to appreciate and accept historic succession as a sign of continuity and of the unity of the church.

In recent years, as a result of ecumenical conversation, Anglicans have been re-examining their understanding of this question in many parts of the world. In 1997, the House of Bishops and the Council of General Synod agreed that the Anglican Church of Canada is prepared to view the historic episcopate in the context of the understandings of apostolicity articulated in *Baptism, Eucharist and Ministry*, *The Niagara Report*, and *The Porvoo Common Statement*, all ecumenical documents that seek to put the episcopate alongside other marks of the apostolicity of the church.

If the Draft Declaration is accepted, both churches will state that they understand the bishops of both churches to be ordained for life service of the gospel in the pastoral ministry of the historic episcopate (cf. Acknowledgements A. 6. c.).

12.   Lutherans wonder, "Will the Declaration change the role of Lutheran bishops?"

The ELCIC has had bishops since its inauguration in 1986, and one of its predecessor bodies has had bishops since 1980. Bishops currently are installed by a liturgical rite that has come to include the laying on of hands by the national bishop and synod bishops. The ELCIC National Convention in 1997 stated that it was prepared to take the constitutional steps necessary to understand the installation of bishops as ordination. Lutherans continue to discuss their understanding of the office of bishop, as they reflect on their relatively new experience of having bishops.

Lutheran bishops in Canada are elected by their synod or national church in convention for a term and they can be re-elected. Lutherans value this polity as keeping bishops accountable. That is one reason why *The Niagara Report* invited churches with lifelong bishops to consider the collegial and periodic review of the bishop's ministry.

Bishops would retain their title, but not exercise jurisdiction, upon retirement, resignation, or completion of their term. This is equivalent to the Anglican situation in which a bishop may resign from jurisdiction but is still considered a bishop. Retired Lutheran bishops may be asked by a synod bishop to perform episcopal functions. Anglican bishops, when they retire or resign, are still bishops, but they may only exercise episcopal ministry by permission of a current diocesan bishop.

The relationship of bishops to pastors and congregations would continue to be governed by the Constitution of the ELCIC. Lutherans have already agreed that only bishops will ordain pastors (cf. *CLAD II, Response to The Niagara Report*, para. 92, received by the National Convention). Although in the Anglican Church of Canada the practice is that only bishops confirm, in the ELCIC, pastors will continue to confirm.

13. Lutherans wonder, "Will the Declaration change the Lutheran understanding of ordained ministry?"

Lutheran understanding of the bishop's ministry is still developing, and different Lutheran churches have responded differently to this question. Lutherans continue to discuss the nature of the ordained ministry. The Declaration asks both churches to acknowledge the full authenticity of each other's ordained ministries as they are presently constituted, without requiring exact agreement about what they mean.

14. Anglicans wonder, "What about the Preface to the Ordinal?"

The present preface in the *Book of Common Prayer* states that "no man shall be accounted or taken to be a lawful bishop, priest or deacon in the Anglican Church of Canada or suffer to execute any of the said functions except he be called, tried, examined and admitted thereunto, according to the form hereafter following, or has had formerly Episcopal consecration or ordination."

The original intent of the preface in 1550 was to stress the continuity of the reformed ministries of the Church of England with their pre-Reformation predecessors. It was not intended to pass judgement on the authenticity of the non-episcopal ministries of the other European reformed churches. In 1661, the phrase "or has had formerly Episcopal consecration or ordination" was added to the preface to resolve the conflict within the Church of England over the episcopate. This later addition, in its historical context, is a statement on the discipline of the Church of England rather than a theological statement on the ministries of other reformed churches.

Some legal experts who have been consulted consider that the matter of the "form hereafter following" was decided by the Supreme Court of Appeal in ruling that the General Synod of the Anglican Church of Canada had the jurisdiction to authorize other liturgies of ordination.

The Draft Declaration would recognize Lutheran bishops as bishops in the church of God; hence they would perform "Episcopal consecration or ordination."

The Chancellor of Nova Scotia advised the Lutheran Relations Task Force that, in his opinion,

> I understand the object is to recognize the validity of the respective ministries to permit legitimate functioning as a priest or minister in either a Lutheran or Anglican setting. It does not appear to me that in order to achieve recognition, any revision to Canons per se are required.

> I would suggest a resolution of General Synod and a separate resolution of the House of Bishops to that effect would be necessary. To permit functioning in any particular Diocese, the permission of the Diocesan Bishop and perhaps a resolution of the Diocesan Synod would also be required.

> It might be argued that recognition of Lutheran ministries would violate the Declaration of Principles ... and the preface to the Ordinal.... This was one of the principal arguments raised before the Supreme Court of Appeal in 1989.... If I am correct in my reading of that decision, the resolutions which I have referred to are probably all that is required. *(letter from Chancellor Carl A. Holm to the Venerable Bud Raymond, 20 October 1993)*

Legislation will be prepared for the 1998 General Synod of the Anglican Church of Canada to consider "on first reading" the changes to canons that would be necessary to implement the Draft Declaration. Dioceses and provinces will then have three years to consider the changes in time for the decisive vote by the General Synod in 2001.

In the case of the churches of North and South India, the Anglican Church of Canada has been prepared to accept the authenticity of all of their clergy, whether or not they have all been, at that point, ordained by bishops in the historic succession.

15. Would we be endangering other ecumenical relationships?

At the national and international levels, Roman Catholics have been partners to the Anglican-Lutheran dialogues. Roman Catholic, Orthodox, Oriental Orthodox, and Protestant churches have been made aware of the state of the dialogue and steps are being taken.

While there has not been any official response, the Pontifical Council for Promoting Christian Unity has been encouraging of Anglican-Lutheran rapprochement, and is itself committed to ecumenical dialogue leading to full visible unity with both of the communions. Roman Catholics and the Orthodox families of churches would not want to see an abandonment of the historic episcopate, but that is not what is being proposed. Rather, both the Anglican and Lutheran communions are taking steps that would broaden the constituency of churches that have the historic episcopate, even though there might be temporary anomalies. There have been temporary anomalies in all our churches.

This is not to take the question lightly. Obviously, if any serious objection were made to the steps being proposed by any other of our dialogue partners, it would have to be treated with an equal seriousness, at the highest levels of decision-making.

16. Are Canadian Anglicans and Lutherans acting alone?

No. The proposals in this country are paralleled by agreements agreed to in Europe and under consideration in the United States, and there are ongoing conversations and common work in other places such as

Namibia, Tanzania, and Malaysia. The process of parallel development of agreements was encouraged by the 1978 Lambeth Conference, which recognized that the peculiar circumstances in different regions of the world would necessitate different steps to reach the same goal.

In fact, the Nordic and Baltic churches (except for Latvia and Denmark), and the churches of Britain and Ireland have endorsed *The Porvoo Common Statement*, and it was implemented in the fall of 1996. The Episcopal Church in the USA voted in July, 1997 to implement the *Concordat of Agreement*. The Evangelical Lutheran Church in America (ELCA) did not approve it, but they have requested that a reworking of the agreement come back to their National Convention in 1999.

The Canadian proposals have been shared with the Ecumenical Officer of the Anglican Consultative Council and with the Ecumenical Advisory Group (ecumenical officers of the provinces of the Communion) at several stages. The Lambeth Conference (1998) and the Anglican Consultative Council (1999) will have an opportunity to comment, if they wish.

The Lutheran World Federation at its meeting in Hong Kong (July, 1997) encouraged Lutheran churches to continue work towards full communion with their Anglican counterparts.

Study Session Outlines

Introduction

Two models of study sessions follow a session for use in one day, and four sessions suitable for use over four weeks.

These study sessions are intended for use by Anglicans and Lutherans together, wherever possible. In situations where this is not practicable, the studies could be used by one church alone.

Members of other churches (e.g., in shared ministry situations), may also wish to take part in the studies. Our hope is that taking this step in our common journey will be of service to the greater unity of the church (Draft Declaration, Preface, 8.).

You will need to have enough copies of the *Lutheran Book of Worship* and the *Book of Alternative Services* or the *Book of Common Prayer* available for all if you choose to compare liturgies, and sufficient copies of the hymns/songs chosen. Please adapt the prayer and song portions to suit your needs and preferences.

One-Day Study

Process

This study is intended to introduce the movement towards full communion to members of the Anglican Church of Canada and the Evangelical Lutheran Church in Canada. Groups who wish to explore the issues in greater depth are encouraged to use the four-session study.

It is expected that a day-long or half-day workshop will be scheduled (suggested time is four hours.) If less time is available, the leaders of the study should choose one of the three focus sections for discussion, i.e., Acknowledgments, Statements, or Commitments. It would be important for participants to read the entire Draft Declaration, including the preface, before the day of the study.

It is suggested that if the study is being held for clergy and laity together, that clergy and laity go into separate small groups.

A form for reporting of issues for further discussion is included with this material. Study leaders are requested to summarize the issues that arise and return the form to their national church office. These responses will guide the development of future studies.

Session

Prayer (10 mins.)

Lutheran Book of Worship (LBW) pp. 161–167
Book of Alternative Services (BAS) pp. 687–697

Song

Bind Us Together (*With One Voice #748*)
Walls That Divide (*Songs for a Gospel People [SGP]*) *#32)*
Many Are the Light Beams (*SGP #104*)
The Church's One Foundation (*Common Praise 1938 #563*)
We Have This Ministry (*SGP #76*)

Introductory Activity (15 mins.)

(in table groups, if the group is large)

Each shares their name, community, and hopes for the day
Each shares a story from their experience of the other's church
Discuss: How are we similar? How are we different?

Biblical Reflection John 17:20–21 (20 mins.)

Discuss: What is your image for the unity that Christ prayed for?
What does it mean to be "one" when we are all so different?
What do you do in your own community to live "as one"?
If Christians were truly "one," what difference might it make?

Presentation of the Declaration (10 mins.)

A leader outlines the history and highlights of the document.

Discussion of the Draft Declaration (3) x (45 mins.)

Acknowledgements
• How do you understand the term "the apostolic faith"?
• How do you understand the term "Sacrament"?
• How do you understand the phrase "personal, collegial and communal oversight"?
• How does the ordained ministry serve the ministry of the whole people of God?

Statements
• What do you understand "ordination" to mean?
• In what ways is authority exercised in your church?
• How are those who exercise leadership kept accountable?
• What does it mean to say that a bishop is "ordained for life service of the Gospel"?
• What does the "Historic Episcopate" mean for your church?

Commitments
• In what ways have we grown together?
• What can we celebrate now?
• What can we do to implement this agreement where we are?

Report Back/Issues Emerging (15 mins.)

• What did you learn?
• What concerns and questions do you have?

Addressing Emerging Issues   (20–30 mins.)

• Questions of fact may be answered by the facilitator
• Critical issues for discussion can be addressed by the group, in table groups, or as a whole
• Sum up with the positive affirmations from the day

Closing Prayer (15 mins.)

A Tale of Two Sisters (p. 38)
Reaffirmation of baptismal bows (pp. 39–42)

Song

The Servant Song *(SGP #133)*
Make Me A Channel of Your Peace *(SGP #2)*
The Beloved Disciple (pp. 43–44)

Additional Activities

Compare baptismal liturgies
Compare ordination rites
Compare eucharistic liturgies
Activities #7, 8, 10, 21 from "Some Things to Do Together" (pp. 45–46)

Four-Session Study

Process

1. The time envisioned for each session is approximately one-and-a half hours. It is important to respect members' needs and commitments by beginning and ending on time.

2. The meeting room should create a welcoming and comfortable atmosphere.

3. The use of music is suggested at the beginning and end of each session. Other appropriate songs and hymns may be used.

4. The group could divide into smaller groups where numbers warrant, especially for discussion of the sections of the Draft Declaration.

5. It will be important to appoint a recorder and to record issues emerging out of the discussion, for feedback to the Joint Working Group. This input will guide the development of future study sessions and contribute to the revision of the Draft Declaration. A form

is provided with this study guide. Please record issues arising in each session and return at the end of the study. We would suggest that the co-ordinator of the study be responsible for doing this.

6. Coffee, tea, and juice might be provided at the beginning or end of each session. If refreshments are served at the end, those who need to leave are free to do so while others may continue conversations.

7. Feel free to adapt the sessions as appropriate for the group concerned.

Session 1: Preface of the Draft Declaration

Opening Prayer

Lutheran Book of Worship (pp. 42–51)
Book of Alternative Services (pp. 676 – 677)

Song

Bind Us Together *(With One Voice #748)*
Walls That Divide *(Songs for a Gospel People [SGP] #32)*
Many Are the Lightbeams *(SGP #104)*

Introductory Activity

(in table groups, if the group is large)

Each shares their name, community, and hopes for the day
Each shares a story from their experience the other's church
Discuss: How are we similar? How are we different?
(describe each in 3 words)

Biblical Perspective John 17:20–21

• What is your picture of the unity Christ prayed for?
• What does it mean to be "one" when we are all so different?

- What do you do in your own community to live "as one"?
- If Christians were truly "one," what difference might it make?

Study of the Draft Declaration

Read:

Preface, paras. 1–4 (pp. 7–8)
Discuss unclear areas, share your understanding of the history

paras 5–6: Movement to Interim Sharing of the Eucharist Agreement to 1995 (pp. 8–9)
Share your experience, if any, with aspects of the agreement

para 7: Definition of Full Communion (p. 9)
Discuss: How close is this definition to the biblical reflection?
How would it help us to bring others to faith?

para 8: Conclusion (p. 13)
What is it in this action that could help other Christian communities?
(local, national, international)

Reporting

Identify and note issues that are raised on the enclosed Response Form

Closing

Litany, *BAS* p. 121

Song

The Beloved Disciple (pp. 43–44)

Additional Activities

Some Things to Do Together #12, 13, 14 (pp. 45–46)
Share the history of your local church

Session 2: Acknowledgements

Opening Prayer

LBW pp. 161–167
BAS pp. 687–689

Song

The Church's One Foundation (*LBW* #369)

Introductory Activity

Question
What is the church for?

Yarn Toss
The first person gives a response to the question and throws a ball of yarn to another person in the group. That person then gives a response. The toss can continue until all have had a chance to comment. The last person can choose to continue the conversation by tossing the yarn on again. People can pass when it is their turn.

Biblical Perspective Ephesians 4:1–7, 11–16

• What does it mean to build up one another in love?
• How do we do that in our families?
• How do we do that in our community?
• How can our churches do that together?

Study of the Draft Declaration

Read *Acknowledgements A. 1.–5.* (pp. 10–11)

Discussion

• How do you understand the term "the apostolic faith"?
• How do you understand the term "Sacrament"?
• How do you understand the phrase "personal, collegial and communal oversight"?

• How does the ordained ministry serve the ministry of the whole people of God?
• How does our understanding of gospel, sacrament and ministry enable the mission of the church?

Additional Activities

Compare baptismal liturgies (*LBW p. 121; BAS p. 152; BCP p. 522*)

Compare worship space: What does it say about our ministry and mission?

Reporting

• What one thing have you learned?
• How can you use this learning?

Closing Prayer

LBW p. 48, *BAS* p. 682 Prayer of St. Francis
BAS p. 676, #2 for the Mission of the Church

Song

The Servant Song (*SGP #133*)

Session 3: Statements

Prayer

LBW pp. 161–167
BAS pp. 687–689

Song

We Have This Ministry (*SGP #76*)

Introduction

What is the anniversary date of your baptism?
How do you celebrate it?

Biblical Perspective

Exodus 19:3–6
I Peter 2:4–10
I Peter 5:1–4

• How do I live out my present ministry as a baptized person?
• How does the ordained ministry serve the priestly ministry of the whole people of God?

Study of the Draft Declaration

Read *Acknowledgements A. 6 a., b., c.* (p. 11)

Discussion

• What do you understand "catholic" and "apostolic" to mean?
• What do you understand "ordination" to mean?
• In what ways is authority exercised in your church?
• How are those who exercise leadership kept accountable?
• What does it mean to say that a bishop is "ordained for life service of the Gospel"?
• What does the "Historic Episcopate" mean for your church?

Additional Activities

Compare ordination rites, especially the examination of the candidate and the prayers

Reporting

• What one thing have you learned?
• How does that help us in our growth towards full communion?

Closing Prayer

Compline
LBW pp. 154–160 *or*
BCP pp. 722–728

Song

Make Me A Channel of Your Peace *(SGP #2)*

Session 4: Commitments

Prayer

LBW pp. 42–51
BAS p. 676 ff.

Song

Thy Hand O God Has Guided *(Common Praise 1938 #561)*
Christ Is the King *(LBW #386)*
In Loving Partnership *(SGP #102)*

Introductory Activity

• How does a stranger become a friend?
• What are the characteristics of true friendship?

Biblical Perspective John 15:15–17

• What does it mean to be friends of Christ?
• What does it mean to be friends in Christ?

Study of the Draft Declaration

Read *Commitments* (pp. 12–13)

Discussion

• What would be different for our two churches if we went ahead:
here in our community; nationally?
• What can we celebrate now?
• What can we look forward to?
• What can we do to implement and live this agreement?

Evaluation

• In what ways have we grown together?
• How have our impressions of one another changed?
• How could these sessions be improved?
• What outstanding issues are there? (please use Report Form)

Additional Activities

"Some Things to Do Together" #7, 8, 21 (pp. 45–46)

Closing

A Tale of Two Sisters (p. 38)
Renewal of baptismal vows (pp. 39–42)

Song

The Beloved Disciple (pp. 43–44)

A Tale of Two Sisters

A Reflection on Christian Unity

There once were two women, living in different countries, who discovered from old records that they were twin sisters. They had been separated when very young and sent to foster families when their own family broke up. Once they contacted each other, they began to write letters, but the letters didn't say very much. Neither of them quite trusted the other; each was afraid that the idea of a twin sister was at best a dream, and at worst some kind of scam.

All that changed when they agreed to meet at their old family home, abandoned now and boarded up since the caretaker had died. They brought a picnic lunch, and as they sat in the garden and ate, their suspicions vanished. Each one, looking at the other under the apple tree, thought she saw herself — not like in a mirror, but in the flesh. They began to laugh together, to tell each other about their lives, their sorrows, their secret hopes.

Then they finally summoned the courage to go into the house. It was dusty, many things were broken, and there were tangles of cobwebs and some scary dark corners. But under the debris they found things: the room they must have shared as infants, with a cot and toys still in it, and even some baby pictures of themselves.

Then, in a few of the pictures, they noticed other children, and in the echoes of their memories they heard the voices of brothers and sisters, laughing and playing. As they cleaned and dusted, they collected all they could find to preserve of the family heritage, and began dreaming of a way to bring children — their own sons and daughters, nieces and nephews — into the old house once again. When they parted, they promised not only to write but to meet again at the house every year; and each swore to do her best to find the other members of their scattered family, and to bring them as well to the next reunion.

The Rev. Iain Luke, Humboldt, Saskatchewan; written for the first joint eucharist between St. John's Nipawin and Beaver Creek Lutheran, 7 November 1993

A Reaffirmation of Baptism

A hymn may be sung at the beginning of the rite. It is suggested that, when possible, a Lutheran and an Anglican preside together as "Presider 1" and "Presider 2." Presider 1 greets the people as follows:

Presider 1   There is one body and one Spirit
All   **There is one hope in God's call to us;**

Presider 1   One Lord, one faith, one baptism,
All   **One God and Father of all.**

The following thanksgiving for water may be sung or said.

Presider 2   Let us give thanks to the Lord our God.
All   **It is right to give God thanks and praise.**

Presider 2   We give you thanks, gracious God, for the gift of water. In the beginning your Spirit moved over the waters. By the gift of water you nourish and sustain the whole creation.
All   **Blessed be God for ever.**

Presider 2   We give you thanks that in water your Son Jesus received the baptism of John and was anointed by the Holy Spirit as the Messiah, the Christ, to lead us, through his death and resurrection, from the bondage of sin into everlasting life. With water Jesus washed the feet of his disciples whom he charged to love one another as he had loved them.
All   **Blessed be God for ever.**

Presider 2   We give you thanks that by water you and the Spirit you have made us a holy priesthood, members of the one body of your Son, Jesus Christ. Pour out your Spirit upon this water that it might be a sign to us of our communion with one another in Jesus Christ our Lord.

All   **Blessed be God for ever.**

Presider 2 We give you thanks and praise and honour and worship through your Servant, Jesus Christ, in the unity of the Holy Spirit, now and for ever.

All   **Blessed are you, our strength and our song, and our salvation.**

Presider 1 My sisters and brothers in Christ, by water and the Holy Spirit God breaks down the walls that divide us and brings us into the household of faith. Let us renew our baptismal promises confident in the unity that is ours in Christ and as our pledge to work to make that unity visible in our time.

Do you reaffirm your renunciation of evil and renew your commitment to Christ?

All   **I do.**

Presider 1 Do you believe in God the Father?

All   **I believe in God,**
the Father almighty,
creator of heaven and earth.

Presider 1 Do you believe in Jesus Christ, the Son of God?

All   **I believe in Jesus Christ,**
his only Son, our Lord.
He was conceived by the power of the Holy
 Spirit
and born of the Virgin Mary.
He suffered under Pontius Pilate,
was crucified, died, and was buried.
He descended to the dead.
On the third day he rose again.
He ascended into heaven,
and is seated at the right hand of the Father.
He will come again
to judge the living and the dead.

Presider 1   Do you believe in God the Holy Spirit?

All   **I believe in the Holy Spirit,
the holy catholic Church,
the communion of saints,
the forgiveness of sins,
the resurrection of the body,
and the life everlasting.**

Presider 2   Will you continue in the apostles' teaching and fellowship, in the breaking of bread, and in the prayers?

All   **I will, with God's help.**

Presider 2   Will you persevere in resisting evil and, whenever you fall into sin, repent and return to the Lord?

All   **I will, with God's help.**

Presider 2   Will you proclaim by Word and example the good news of God in Christ?

All   **I will, with God's help.**

Presider 2   Will you seek and serve Christ in all persons, loving your neighbour as yourself?

All   **I will, with God's help.**

Presider 2   Will you strive for justice and peace among all people, and respect the dignity of every human being?

All   **I will, with God's help.**

One or both of the presiders may sprinkle the gathered people with the blessed water, or one may invite the people to come forward to sign themselves or each other with the water.

Presider 1   Gracious Lord, through water and the Spirit you have made us your own. You forgave us all our sins and brought us to newness of life. Continue to strengthen us with the Holy Spirit, and daily increase in us your gifts of grace: the spirit of wisdom and understanding, the spirit of counsel

and might, the spirit of knowledge and the fear
of the Lord, the spirit of joy in your presence;
through Jesus Christ, your Son, our Lord.

All   **Amen.**

Presider 2   Being made one by the power of the Holy Spirit,
let us pray as our Saviour taught us:

All   **Our Father in heaven,**
hallowed be your name,
your kingdom come,
your will be done,
on earth as in heaven.
Give us today our daily bread.
Forgive us our sins
as we forgive those who sin against us.
Save us from the time of trial,
and deliver us from evil.
For the kingdom, the power,
and the glory are yours,
now and for ever. Amen.

A hymn may be sung.

To conclude the service, the following may be said.

All   **The grace of our Lord Jesus Christ, and the love of**
God, and the fellowship of the Holy Spirit, be with
us all evermore. Amen.

The Beloved Disciple

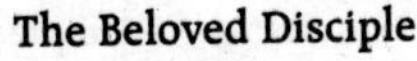

The Beloved Disciple

Some Things to Do Together

1. Discuss the paragraphs from *Baptism, Eucharist and Ministry* together (pp. 67–70).

2. Compare each other's liturgies, particularly the Eucharist and ordination rites.

3. Describe how bishops function, noting similarities and differences.

4. Explain to each other how major decisions are made by the whole church.

5. Study the lections for Sunday.

6. What early impressions did you have of the Lutheran/Anglican churches?

7. Discuss the current needs of your community and identify resources for common outreach.

8. Undertake a joint project in your community

9. Study the *Augsburg Confession* and the *Thirty-Nine Articles*.

10. Discuss the definition of full communion. Is this something you want?

11. Pray.

12. Share the history of the founding of your parish or congregation. What major issues was the church struggling with at that time?

13. Share the story of your journey in faith.

14. Identify gifts you see in the other that you and your church need.

15. Celebrate the eucharist.

16. Share in joint Lenten programs, or exchange parish worship on All Saints', Ash Wednesday, Good Friday, Ascension Day, or a day of local significance.

17. Have a skit night, focusing on your history or customs.

18. Share meals.

19. Arrange for joint meetings, projects, retreats or outings for groups of similar interest (e.g., youth, women, seniors, choirs).

20. Host a neighbourhood party.

21. Consider everything you do as a congregation and ask yourselves, "Couldn't we do this together?"

WHO WE ARE

The Evangelical Lutheran Church in Canada

The Evangelical Lutheran Church in Canada (ELCIC) came into being January 1, 1986, the result of a merger between The Evangelical Lutheran Church of Canada (ELCC) and the Canada Section of the Lutheran Church in America. The ELCC (formerly the Canada District of The American Lutheran Church) had been formed as an autonomous church in Canada in 1967 and was joined by the Eastern Conference of the former Canada District in 1968.

ELCIC membership comprises 196,393 baptized members gathered in 642 congregations in 8 provinces and 2 territories of Canada (there are no ELCIC congregations in Newfoundland or Prince Edward Island).

There are 5 regional synods: British Columbia (16,000 members); Alberta and the Territories (43,000); Saskatchewan (37,000); Manitoba (24,000); and Eastern Canada (77,000).

The ELCIC is a member church of the Lutheran World Federation (LWF), World Council of Churches, Canadian Council of Churches, and the Lutheran Council in Canada (which is the forum for bilateral cooperation with Lutheran Church-Canada, the LC-C). Mission and development with overseas churches is done cooperatively with the LWF and with the LC-C through Canadian Lutheran World Relief (CLWR). In addition, the ELCIC supports twelve missionary units and volunteer in mission units serving in partner churches in nine countries. The ELCIC works cooperatively with ecumenical coalitions in Canada in advocacy and justice.

The ELCIC currently has approximately 635 active clergy serving as follows: 480 parish pastors; 5 missionaries; 13 campus chaplains; 1 military chaplain; 10 correctional chaplains; 38 hospital chaplains; and the rest serving in specialized ministries (e.g., professors, bishops, administrators, counselors). The ELCIC relates to two seminaries (in Saskatoon and Waterloo), two colleges, and two high schools.

The ELCIC meets in biennial conventions in odd-numbered years, with each parish represented by one delegate and entitled to a second (lay) delegate if its baptized membership is over 800. There are 200 clergy delegates and approximately 300 lay delegates. The purpose of conventions is for business and fellowship. There is a National Church Council of 20 members, including four officers, three of whom serve full-time in office. The Vice-President is a volunteer. The national bishop is chief pastor and chief executive officer. All officers serve renewable terms of four years. Synod bishops serve as advisory members to National Church Council.

The five regional synods have responsibility for implementing the mission of the church within their territories, and for shepherding congregations and pastors. Each synod has four elected officers (with only the bishop serving full-time in office) and an elected synod council. Synods meet in biennial conventions in the year between national conventions. The synods are further divided into conferences for the purpose of fellowship, study, and implementing mission.

The flow of benevolence funds is from congregations to synods to national church. There are requested benevolence commitments, but there are no binding assessments or commitments.

The ELCIC relates to the Evangelical Lutheran Women, Inc. and to ELCIC Group Services, Inc., which manages the church's pension and benefits plan.

The largest gathering of the ELCIC is the Canadian Lutheran Youth Gathering, involving up to 1,600 youth and adults meeting biennially for inspiration, study, worship, and celebration.

Ministry Areas in the Evangelical Lutheran Church in Canada

The ELCIC identifies five ministry areas in which the church will seek to grow in fulfillment of its mission to share the gospel of Jesus Christ in our world in this time and place. Support to develop ministry in the five areas is provided through ELCIC staff, budget dollars, and working groups, which engage synod representatives in churchwide planning, consultation, and coordination. The Working Groups have responsibility for planning and guiding national ministries in the ar-

Response Form

(tear out)

RESPONSE FORM

At the conclusion of the study, please return this form to your national church office (addresses on other side).

THE JOINT DECLARATION

Under the following headings, please list the most important issues raised during your discussion.

Preface (Joint Declaration)

Acknowledgements (Joint Declaration A. 1.–5.)

Statements (Joint Declaration A. 6.)

Commitments (Joint Declaration C.)

Please summarize any other concerns you have.

THE STUDY GUIDE

What did you find helpful in this study material and process?

How would you improve the study material and process?

NATIONAL OFFICE CONTACTS

At the conclusion of the study, please return this form to your national office

The Rev. Cindy Halmarson
Evangelical Lutheran Church in Canada
500 Portage Avenue, 4th Floor
Winnipeg, MB R3C 3X1

The Rev. Canon Alyson Barnett-Cowan
Anglican Church of Canada
600 Jarvis Street
Toronto, Ontario M4Y 2J6

eas of Discipleship, Faith and Society, Leadership for Ministry, Mission, and Worship.

Discipleship

The ELCIC is committed to equip people for mission and discipleship by assisting them to be disciples who talk about their faith and help others in Christ's name. We will involve all the baptized at all stages and circumstances of their lives in the development of skills and training; identification and use of resources; and equipping them to use their own gifts and talents while also developing, nurturing, and using the gifts of others.

Programmatic areas in Discipleship include: the adult catechumenate, lay leadership training, learning, witness, youth, outdoor, and family ministries.

Faith and Society

The ELCIC is committed to the mission of God, which takes seriously the reality of the world and the reality of Christ with equal care. We commit ourselves to encourage companionship and advocacy with those who are treated unjustly. This means that we will model the reign of God in our walking with and advocacy for the poor and marginalized; actively working for justice and peace; preparing ourselves for companionship and advocacy; encouraging our national church to struggle with ethical and moral issues and to speak out clearly and prophetically; and working cooperatively with others.

Programmatic areas in Faith and Society include: research, policy development, support and cooperative work with ecumenical coalitions, and addressing issues of church and society.

Leadership for Ministry

Within the priesthood of believers, leaders in ministry are identified, trained, and nurtured for ordained, diaconal, and other ministries. We commit ourselves to develop and foster leadership in our church. This means that we will set standards for called, ordained, and commissioned leaders; review our church's understanding and practice of ordained, diaconal, and other ministers; and strengthen our ongoing support of leaders for ministry.

Programmatic areas in Leadership and Ministry include: supporting coordination of seminaries and synod preparation committees, establishing and maintaining standards for ordination, policy development, and recruitment for ministry.

Mission

The Holy Spirit calls and gathers the whole church into the mission of God found on our doorsteps and around the world. We commit ourselves to respond to the many opportunities for mission and to pursue creative and effective ways for mission and ministry in our local, national, and global communities. This means placing a high priority on openness to new and ongoing opportunities for mission and ministry as needs arise and are identified.

Programmatic areas in Mission include: campus ministry, global mission, mission in Canada, and volunteers in mission.

Worship

We commit ourselves to worship the Triune God through Word and Sacrament. This means that worship in our church will proclaim the gospel and uphold the theology of the cross; be hospitable and nurturing to all; be faithful to Scripture and the Lutheran Confessions; be relevant and meaningful in a variety of contexts; and involve laity and clergy working together.

Programmatic areas in Worship include: training for worship leadership; attention to spiritual formation and nurture; attention to the arts; development of resource material; and recommending policies and standards.

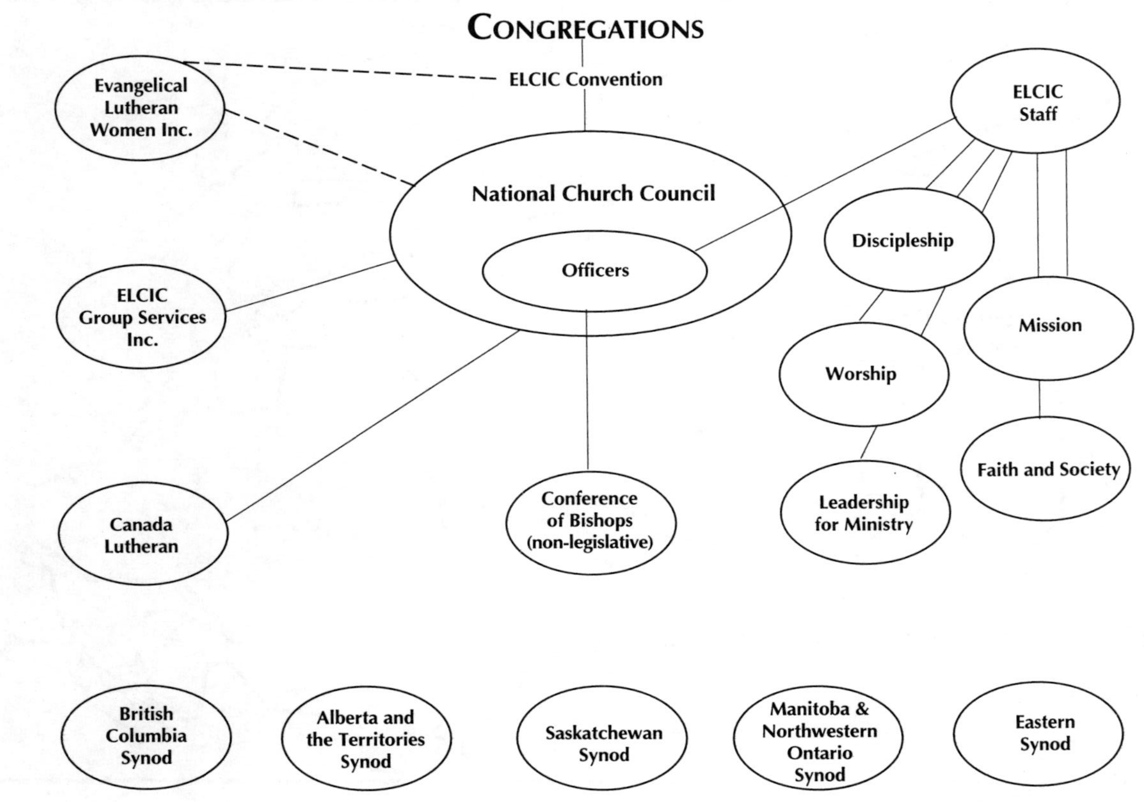

CONGREGATIONS
ELCIC Convention
Evangelical Lutheran Women Inc.
National Church Council
Officers
ELCIC Staff
Discipleship
Mission
Worship
Faith and Society
Leadership for Ministry
ELCIC Group Services Inc.
Conference of Bishops (non-legislative)
Canada Lutheran
British Columbia Synod
Alberta and the Territories Synod
Saskatchewan Synod
Manitoba & Northwestern Ontario Synod
Eastern Synod

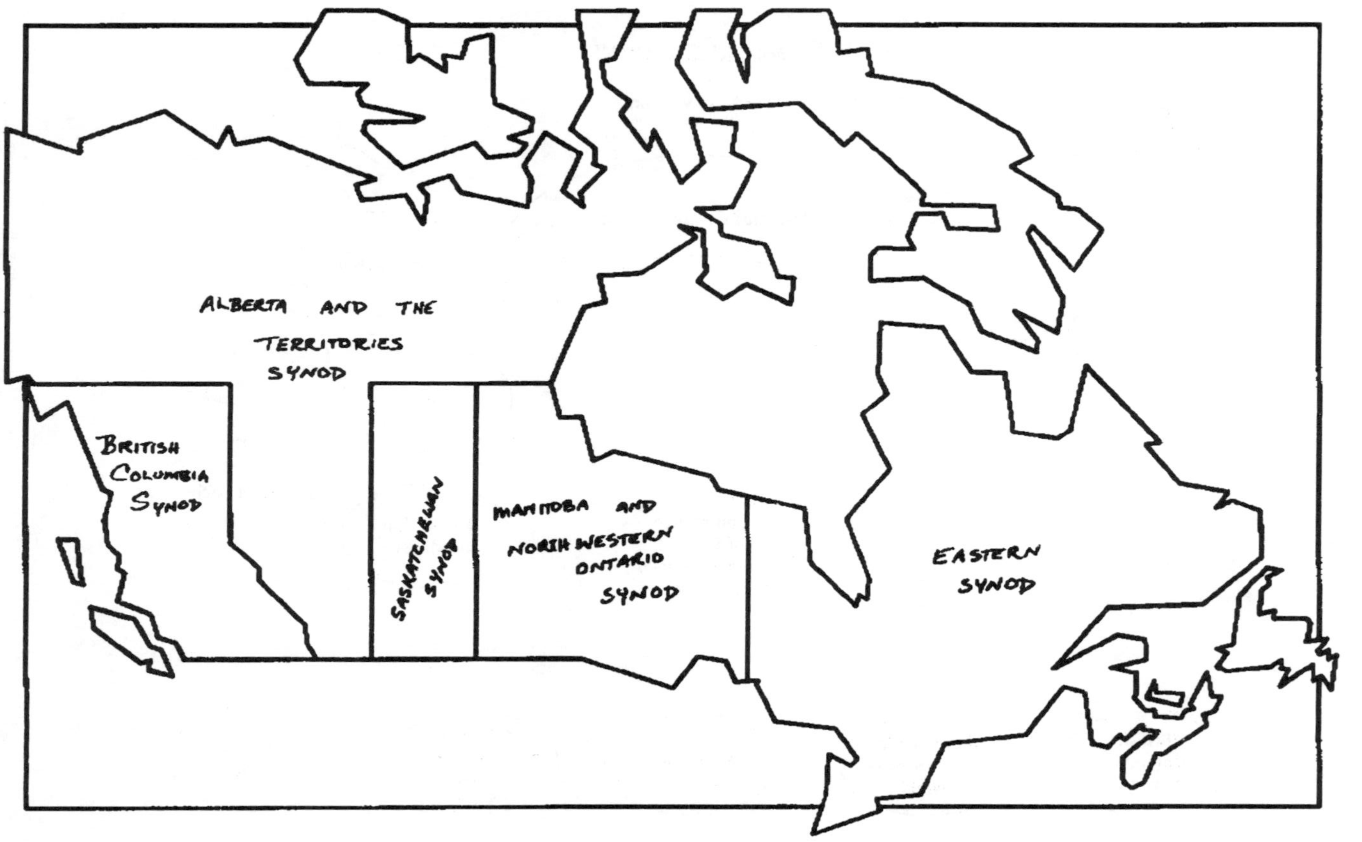
ALBERTA AND THE TERRITORIES SYNOD
BRITISH COLUMBIA SYNOD
SASKATCHEWAN SYNOD
MANITOBA AND NORTH WESTERN ONTARIO SYNOD
EASTERN SYNOD

The Anglican Church of Canada

Population of Canada: 27,000,000 (1991 census, rounded up)
Number of Anglicans: 2,188,115 (1991 census); 740,262 (parish rolls)

Dioceses: 30 dioceses grouped into four internal ecclesiastical provinces (i.e., Canada, Ontario, Rupert's Land, and British Columbia and Yukon)

Parishes: 1,850
Congregations: 2,390
Number of clergy (active and retired): 3,306; active: 2,023
Number of bishops (active and retired): 80; active: 42

Brief History: The first Anglican worship service in what is now Canada took place when the Rev. Robert Wolfall, chaplain to Sir Martin Frobisher's third Arctic expedition, celebrated the eucharist on 22 July 1578. The first regular church services in mainland Canada were held in 1710 at Port Royal, Nova Scotia. The first church building, St. Paul's in Halifax, was built in 1750 and Bishop Charles Inglis was consecrated the first bishop of the diocese of Nova Scotia in 1787. Much of the early work of establishing and serving churches and missions in Canada was the result of British church and missionary societies, including the Society for the Propagation of the Gospel (SPG) and the Church Missionary Society (CMS). In 1893, the several dioceses of the Canadian church came together to form the first General Synod of the Anglican Church of Canada (then called the Church of England in Canada) led by the Primate, elected from the House of Bishops. In 1924, with the admission of Newfoundland (25 years before it joined Confederation in 1949), General Synod became a national body encompassing the whole of the Anglican Church in Canada from coast to coast.
Today the Anglican Church of Canada (the name was changed in 1955) stretches from east to west and north beyond the Arctic Circle. It is home to worshippers from many cultural and ethnic backgrounds, including significant numbers of Canada's First Nations peoples. The

Anglican Church of Canada has a long history of involvement with Aboriginal peoples and has recently entered into a covenant relationship to create a new partnership.

The first element of the Anglican Church's Mission Statement declares that its primary purpose is to "proclaim and celebrate the gospel of Jesus Christ in worship and action." The standards for Anglican worship are found in two liturgical texts: the *Book of Common Prayer* (BCP 1962) and the *Book of Alternative Services* (BAS 1985). A new hymn book (*Common Praise*) is in preparation and will be available in 1998.

The Anglican Church of Canada preserves the three-fold order of ministry, with deacons, priests, and bishops. In 1976, after several years of study and legislative debate, the church ordained the first women to the priesthood in Canada. In 1993, the Rt. Rev. Victoria Matthews was elected the first Canadian Anglican woman bishop.

In addition to its mission and evangelism work, the Anglican Church of Canada has a strong commitment to advocacy, social justice, and disaster relief. As well as its active participation in a number of inter-church coalition, the Anglican Church includes the work of the Primate's World Relief and Development Fund (PWRDF). The Fund was established in 1959 in response to the Springhill Mining Disaster but today is active worldwide.

The Anglican Church of Canada has long been committed to Christian dialogue. It was a founding member of the Canadian Council of Churches in 1944 and the World Council of Churches in 1948. The General Synod of the Anglican Church of Canada entered into An Agreement on the Interim Sharing of the Eucharist with the Evangelical Lutheran Church in Canada in 1989 and is currently active in the Anglican/Roman Catholic Dialogue in Canada.

Internationally, the Anglican Church of Canada is a member of the worldwide Anglican Communion, headed (*primus inter pares*) by the Archbishop of Canterbury, currently, the Most Rev. and Rt. Hon. Dr. George Carey. The Communion is involved in a number of ongoing dialogues with the Roman Catholic, Orthodox, Oriental Orthodox and Methodist churches. Anglican-Lutheran dialogue and agreement have been especially rich. In northern Europe, Anglicans and Lutherans already share a relationship of full communion.

Mission Statement of the Anglican Church of Canada

As a partner in the worldwide Anglican Communion and in the universal church, we proclaim and celebrate the gospel of Jesus Christ in worship and action.

We value our heritage of biblical faith, reason, liturgy, tradition, bishops and synods, and the rich variety of our life in community.

We acknowledge that God is calling us to greater diversity of membership, wider participation in ministry and leadership, better stewardship in God's creation and a strong resolve in challenging attitudes and structures that cause injustice.

Guided by the Holy Spirit, we commit ourselves to respond to this call in love and service and so more fully live the life of Christ.

Strategic Plan for Work at the National Level

In 1995, General Synod adopted a 9-year Strategic Plan, which set priorities and ways of working. The priorities are:

1. Strengthen our mission and development partnerships outside Canada.

In accordance with the Anglican Communion's 10 Principles of Partnership, seek to learn from our partners and focus our resources to enable local autonomy.
   a. Create stronger mutually beneficial worldwide partnerships
   b. Target specific regions overseas for priority partnership work (e.g., Tanzania)
   c. Link companion dioceses to targeted regions
   d. Expand Volunteers in Mission with increased educational component

e. Provide funds to the extent possible
f. Facilitate networks for education and advocacy
g. Increase collaboration between committees engaged in international work (e.g., fundraising, education, networking, and advocacy)

2. Clarify Anglican identity, liturgy, and worship.

Coordinate standards for worship, liturgy, and ministry; provide liturgical resources; promote networks.
a. Primacy promoted as focus of unity
b. Articulate standards for public worship
c. Develop liturgical resources, sensitive to a multicultural context
d. Facilitate consultations regarding liturgy
e. Research theological/ethical issues to share with dioceses
f. Participate in the Anglican Consultative Council and fund to the extent possible
g. Foster and facilitate collaboration between Canadian theological colleges and between the national church and the colleges
h. Journey with indigenous peoples

3. Nurture ecumenical relationships.

Engage in ecumenical discussion and activity.
a. Use the Lund Principle — work ecumenically wherever possible
b. Participate in the World Council of Churches and Canadian Council of Churches and fund to the extent possible
c. Engage in ecumenical/interfaith dialogues

4. Advocate social justice and prophetic mission within Canada, especially in indigenous peoples' concerns and social and economic justice issues.

Concentrate on the promotion of networks and develop discussion frameworks; develop a new relationship with indigenous peoples.

a. Build, facilitate, and animate coordinated networks in partnership with dioceses
b. Initiate development of frameworks to engage people in ethical reflection
c. Participate in ecumenically-based research, advocacy, and educational activities (i.e., through restructured coalitions)
d. Guide national/diocesan relationships using partnership principles
e. Develop targeted communications to enable better informed networks (e.g., downlinks, computer networks)
f. Journey with indigenous peoples towards healing and reconciliation

5. Strengthen commitment of the whole church to domestic mission in partnership with the Council of the North and work with the Council of the North towards self-sufficiency.

Coordinate transfer payments and encourage improvements in stewardship
a. Identify needs not currently being met
b. Encourage increased stewardship education in assisted dioceses
c. Continue to develop Anglican Appeal partially for the Council of the North

6. Provide services to dioceses — information, financial, administration.

Provide and share expertise; coordinate communication.
a. Provide information and communication services (research, resources, publishing, archives) to dioceses and to the national church to support the priorities
b. Affirm *The Journal's* primary responsibility "...to inform Anglicans in Canada about the domestic and international work of their church..." within the context of a coordinated national communications approach. The independent editorial policy continues
c. Facilitate networks of finance officers and financial development volunteers

   d. Provide expertise and availability in pensions, administrative services, financial development, and gift planning

   e. Proposals for a coordinated national fundraising capability need to be developed and tailored to suit the needs of parishes, dioceses, and the national church, and focused on the priorities in this option

   f. Develop a volunteer and staff resource capacity to assist dioceses in handling financial/legal/communications/ personnel/ property issues

7. Eliminate other nationally coordinated domestic mission.

No national program support.

   a. Eliminate all program development, resource production, consultation other than that required for the above (e.g., congregational development, youth ministry, stewardship education)

Structure

General Synod meets every three years. It has three houses: of bishops, of clergy, and of laity, but all meet together. Each diocese is represented by an equal number of clergy and laity, with the number being related to the Anglican population of the diocese. The Primate is the President of the General Synod and of the House of Bishops. The Prolocutor, elected by the clergy and lay members of General Synod, shares in the leadership of the Synod. Other officers include the General Secretary, Chancellor, and Deputy Prolocutor (there is currently a review of the number of officers).

The priorities of General Synod are promoted and monitored by the Council of General Synod, which is made up of 40 representatives, including one from each diocese. The Council oversees seven committees and two councils. The Committees are Primate's World Relief and Development (PWRDF), Partners in Mission, Faith Worship and Ministry, Information Resources, Financial Management and Development, Pensions, and Eco-Justice. The Councils are the Council of the North (assisted dioceses) and the Anglican Council of Indigenous Peoples.

ORGANIZATIONAL STRUCTURE – OVERVIEW

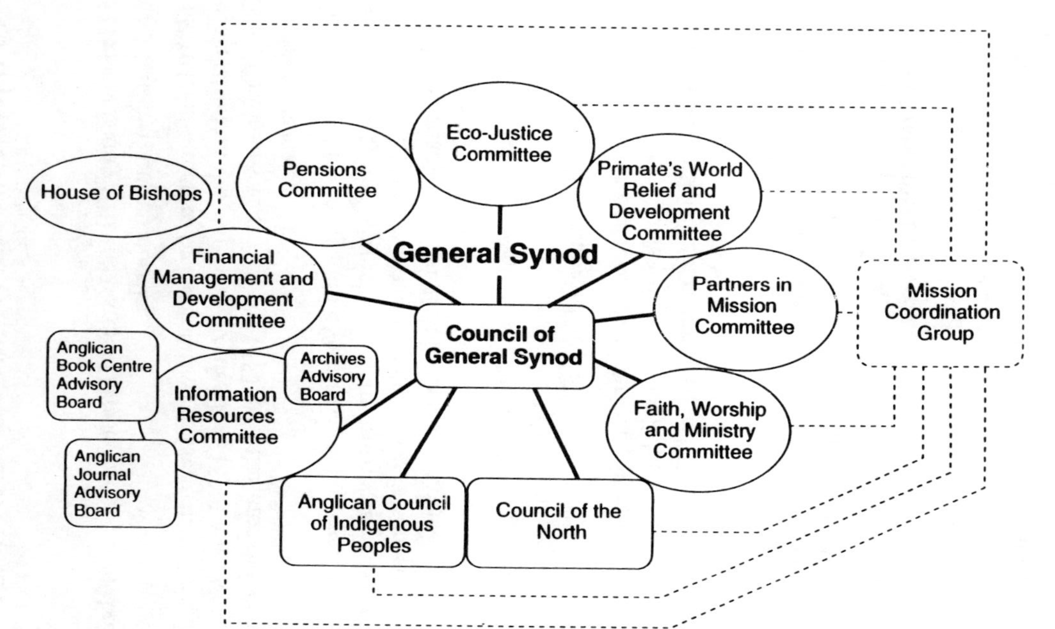

Passed by General Synod, June 1995

Dates of Interest in Anglican-Lutheran Relations

May, 1521: King Henry VIII and Cardinal Wolsey preside at the burning of a collection of Luther's books.

1538: 13 Articles agreed to by a committee of German and English theologians; based on the Augsburg Confession (1530), they serve as the basis for Cranmer's 42 Articles of 1553, and thus, for the *Thirty-Nine Articles of Religion*.

1709: Society for the Propagation of Christian Knowledge (SPCK) takes responsibility for Danish-German Lutheran Mission at Tranquebar, India. Continues to use Lutheran pastors, some of whom served as salaried chaplains of the East India Company using the *Book of Common Prayer*, till 1825.

1841: England and Prussia jointly establish the Jerusalem bishopric and Michael Solomon Alexander consecrated first bishop on November 7. Joint sponsorship terminated in 1886.

1888: Lambeth Conference receives initiative of Swedish Church to explore differences with a view to the establishment of intercommunion, if possible. Official report appeared in 1911, recommending intercommunion.

1920: Lambeth Conference encourages adoption of the report's recommendations. Two Anglican bishops participate in the consecration of two Swedish bishops at Uppsala, on 19 September 1920.

1927: Swedish bishop participates in the consecration of three Anglican bishops at Canterbury 1 November.

1930: Lambeth Conference extends conversations to include the Church of Finland, and, later, the churches of Estonia and Latvia. First Anglican bishop participates in a consecration of a Finnish bishop in 1951. First participation by an Anglican bishop in a Baltic consecration occurs in 1989.

1969: Lutheran-Episcopal Dialogue begins in the United States of America. First Progress Report published in 1973 (LED I).

1970-72: First Communion-wide dialogue between churches of the Anglican Communion and churches of the Lutheran World Federation. Pullach Report issued in 1973.

1975: Anglican-Lutheran Working Group recommends regional dialogues in North America, Africa, and Europe.

1976-1980: Second series of Lutheran-Episcopal Dialogues in the USA.

1980-82: Anglican-Lutheran European Regional Commission meets and issues the Helsinki Report, which saw "no serious obstacles on the way to the establishment of full communion."

Agreement on Interim Sharing of the Eucharist between the Episcopal Church of the USA and the Lutheran Church of America, the American Lutheran Church, and the Association of Evangelical Lutheran Churches. (These Lutheran Churches merged in 1988 to form the Evangelical Lutheran Church in America.)

1983: Anglican-Lutheran Joint Working Group calls for the establishment of a permanent Continuation Committee to oversee and further Anglican-Lutheran relations internationally.

The Cold Ash Report, offering a definition of full communion, is issued.

Canadian church leaders call for the establishment of Lutheran Anglican Dialogue.

1986: Canadian Lutheran-Anglican Dialogue (CLAD I) issues *Report and Recommendations*, declaring agreement in the faith and calling for extensive cooperation between the two churches, including an interim agreement on sharing the eucharist.

Anglican-Lutheran International Continuation Committee (ALICC) established; name later changed to Anglican-Lutheran International Commission.

1987: ALICC holds international consultation on *Episcope* and issues *The Niagara Report*.

1988: The Church of England and the Evangelical Lutheran Church in Germany (EKD) issue *On the Way to Visible Unity: The Meissen Report;* report comes into effect in 1992.

1989: Anglican Church of Canada and the Evangelical Lutheran Church in Canada adopt Agreement on Interim Sharing of the Eucharist.

Talks between the churches of England, Ireland, Scotland, and Wales and all the Nordic and Baltic churches begin.

1991: *Towards Full Communion* and *Concordat of Agreement* between the Evangelical Lutheran Church in America and the Episcopal Church of the United States of America published.

1992: Canadian Lutheran-Anglican Dialogue (CLAD II) publishes *Response to The Niagara Report.*

1993: Nordic, Baltic, British, and Irish conversations lead to the publication of *Together in Mission and Ministry*, including *The Porvoo Common Statement*, which would lead to a relationship of full communion and mutual recognition of ministries among the churches.

1995: Evaluation of Canada's Agreement on Interim Sharing of the Eucharist calls for mutual recognition of each other's members without requiring re-confirmation, and extends the possibilities for pastors/priests to serve in each other's churches when both bishops agree. Joint Working Group established to bring forward proposals for full communion by 2001.

1996: Nordic churches (except the Church of Denmark), Baltic churches (except the Church of Latvia), and the churches of Britain and Ireland agree to *The Porvoo Common Statement.* Agreement celebrated in Trondheim, Westminster, and Riga.

1997: General Convention of the Episcopal Church of America endorses the *Concordat of Agreement;* the Evangelical Lutheran Church of America fails to pass it by 6 votes less than the required two-thirds majority. A rewrite of the agreement is called for.

The Canadian Anglican House of Bishops and the Council of General Synod agree that they are prepared to view the historic episcopate in the context of the understandings of apostolicity articulated in *Baptism, Eucharist and Ministry, The Niagara Report*, and *The Porvoo*

Common Statement. The National Convention of the Evangelical Lutheran Church in Canada agrees that it is prepared to take the constitutional steps necessary to understand the installation of synodical bishops as ordination. The National Church Council of the ELCIC and the Council of General Synod of the ACC agree that the Draft Declaration should be widely circulated for study in the two churches.

KEY DOCUMENTS

1. "Towards Full Communion: Anglicans and Lutherans in Canada"

A resource produced by the Lutheran Relations Task Force of the Inter-Church Inter-Faith Relations Committee in preparation for the 1995 General Synod. Distributed at General Synod as a supplement to the Report of ICIFRC (*an 8-page 8 x 11 brochure containing the text of the resolution that was subsequently adopted by both General Synod and the National Convention of the ELCIC, together with the text of the Interim Sharing of the Eucharist Agreement, the working definition of "full communion," and some background reflection pieces*).

2. Report to the 1995 General Synod of the Inter-Church Inter-Faith Relations Committee

In the Convening Circular for the 1995 Synod. (*Contains the history of the development of the relationship to date, together with the rationale for the 1995 resolutions.*)

3. Interim Sharing of the Eucharist: Introduction and Commentary

The text of the 1989 agreement and background information about how it came about; some guidelines for its implementation. Available from the Resource Centre at 600 Jarvis St., Toronto, ON M4Y 2J6; tel. (416) 924-9199 ext. 317. (*Note that this commentary is on the version of the agreement before it was amended in 1995. The amended version of the agreement, without commentary, is part, of this resource package.*)

4. CLAD I: Report and Recommendations, April, 1986

The final report from the first round of the Canadian Lutheran-Anglican Dialogue. Available from the Resource Centre at 600 Jarvis St., Toronto, ON M4Y 2J6; tel. (416) 924-9199 ext. 317. (*Contains the background to the dialogue; Agreed Statements on Justification, the Eucha-*

rist, Apostolicity, and the Ordained Ministry; recommendations that became the basis for the 1989 Interim Sharing of the Eucharist Agreement.)

5. The Niagara Report

The report of the September, 1987 consultation on *episcope* held by the Anglican-Lutheran International Continuation Committee. Published by Church House (London) and Forward Movement Publications (Cincinnati) in 1988. (*Important joint statement on episcope and its exercise; contains invitations to both churches to take certain steps to enable agreement on episcopal ministry; paragraphs 89–92 addressed to Lutherans, and paragraphs 94–96 addressed to Anglicans.*)

6. CLAD II: Response to The Niagara Report

A 1992 joint response to the paragraphs of Niagara noted above. Available from the Resource Centre, 600 Jarvis St., Toronto, ON M4Y 2J5; tel. (416) 924-9199 ext. 317. (*This response was adopted by the ELCIC at its 1993 National Convention; consultation among Anglicans is ongoing, and led to the 1995 resolutions.*)

7. "Towards Full Communion" and "Concordat of Agreement"

The report of the American Lutheran Episcopal Dialogue, Series III; Minneapolis: Augsburg, 1991. (*Contains background information on the dialogue process in the USA between the Episcopal Church and the Evangelical Lutheran Church in America. The precise proposals to implement full communion [which would involve Episcopalians suspending the Preface to the Ordinal, and Lutherans not requiring Episcopal clergy to subscribe to the Augsburg Confession] were approved by the Episcopal Church but narrowly rejected by the ELCA in the summer of 1997. A further agreement will be sought to bring back in 1999/2000.*)

8. Together in Mission and Ministry ("Porvoo")

The Porvoo Common Statement with Essays on Church and Ministry in Northern Europe: conversations between the British and Irish Anglican churches and the Nordic and Baltic Lutheran churches. (*The agreed statement that has now been ratified by all but the Danish and Latvian churches, and that was implemented in the fall of 1996. Includes important work on apostolicity and historic succession, and background information on episcopacy in all the churches involved.)*

9. Baptism, Eucharist and Ministry (BEM)

The key ecumenical document of recent history, Faith and Order Paper 111 (Geneva, WCC, 1982). *(Paragraphs 34–38 and 51–53 of the section on Ministry underlie much of the discussion about episcopacy and mutual recognition of ministries. The statement on apostolicity is widely regarded as the heart of agreed statements on the subject in ecumenical dialogue. BEM was a very important impetus in the renewal of Anglican-Lutheran dialogue throughout the world, and has been an incentive for all Lutheran churches of the Lutheran World Federation to move towards adopting the episcopate.)*

10. The Diaconate as Ecumenical Opportunity

The Hanover Report of the Angican Lutheran International Commission. London: Anglican Communion Publications, 1996. The diaconate challenges both Lutherans and Anglicans to explore and clarify alternative forms of ministry that are distinct from parish or pastoral leadership. The international commission has grappled with practices and assumptions about the diaconate in each of their traditions. In doing so, they have addressed questions of ecclesiology, liturgy, and ministry and ordination, and opened many helpful ways forward. The diaconate presents an opportunity to continue to dialogue and cooperated ecumenically, and we expect the exploration to continue both internationally and in Canada.

Baptism, Eucharist and Ministry: Statement on Ministry (Excerpts)

III. The Forms of the Ordained Ministry

C. Functions of Bishops, Presbyters and Deacons

29. *Bishops* preach the Word, preside at the sacraments, and administer discipline in such a way as to be representative pastoral ministers of oversight, continuity and unity in the Church. They have pastoral oversight of the area to which they are called. They serve the apostolicity and unity of the Church's teaching, worship and sacramental life. They have responsibility for leadership in the Church's mission. They relate the Christian community in their area to the wider Church and the universal Church to their community. They, in communion with the presbyters and deacons and the whole community, are responsible for the orderly transfer of ministerial authority in the Church.

IV. Succession in the Apostolic Tradition

A. Apostolic Tradition in the Church

34. In the Creed, the Church confesses itself to be apostolic. The Church lives in continuity with the apostles and their proclamation. The same Lord who sent the apostles continues to be present in the Church. The Spirit keeps the Church in the apostolic tradition until the fulfillment of history in the Kingdom of God. Apostolic tradition in the Church means continuity in the permanent characteristics of the Church of the apostles; witness to the apostolic faith, proclamation and fresh interpretation of the Gospel, celebration of baptism and the eucharist, the transmission of ministerial responsibilities, communion in prayer, love, joy and suffering, service to the sick and the

needy, unity among the local churches and sharing the gifts which the Lord has given to each.

B. Succession of the Apostolic Ministry

35. The primary manifestation of apostolic succession is to be found in the apostolic tradition of the Church as a whole. The succession is an expression of the permanence, and, therefore, of the continuity of Christ's own mission in which the Church participates. Within the Church the ordained ministry has a particular task of preserving and actualizing the apostolic faith. The orderly transmission of the ordained ministry is therefore a powerful expression of the continuity of the Church throughout history; it also underlines the calling of the ordained minister as guardian of the faith. Where churches see little importance in orderly transmission, they should ask themselves whether they have not to change their conception of continuity in the apostolic tradition. On the other hand, where the ordained ministry does not adequately serve the proclamation of the apostolic faith, churches must ask themselves whether their ministerial structures are not in need of reform.

36. Under the particular historic circumstances of the growing Church in the early centuries, the succession of bishops became one of the ways, together with the transmission of the Gospel and the life of the community, in which the apostolic tradition of the Church was expressed. This succession was understood as serving, symbolizing and guarding the continuity of the apostolic faith and communion.

37. In churches which practice the succession through the episcopate, it is increasingly recognized that a continuity in apostolic faith, worship and mission has been preserved in churches which have not retained the form of historic episcopate. This recognition finds additional support in the fact that the reality and function of the episcopal ministry have been preserved in many of these churches, with or without the title "bishop". Ordination, for example, is always done in them by persons in whom the Church recognizes the authority to transmit the ministerial commission.

38. These considerations do not diminish the importance of the episcopal ministry. On the contrary, they enable churches which have not retained the episcopate to appreciate the episcopal succession as a sign, though not a guarantee, of the continuity and unity of the Church. Today churches, including those engaged in union negotiations, are expressing willingness to accept episcopal succession as a sign of the apostolicity of the life of the whole Church. Yet, at the same time, they cannot accept any suggestion that the ministry exercised in their own tradition should be invalid until the moment that it enters into an existing line of episcopal succession. Their acceptance of the episcopal succession will best further the unity of the whole Church if it is par of a wider process by which the episcopal churches themselves also regain their lost unity.

VI. Towards the Mutual Recognition of the Ordained Ministries

51. In order to advance towards the mutual recognition of ministries, deliberate efforts are required. All churches need to examine the forms of ordained ministry and the degree to which the churches are faithful to its original intentions. Churches must be prepared to renew their understanding and their practice of the ordained ministry.

52. Among the issues that need to be worked on as churches move towards mutual recognition of ministries, that of apostolic succession is of particular importance. Churches in ecumenical conversations can recognize their respective ordained ministries if they are mutually assured of their intention to transmit the ministry of Word and Sacrament in continuity with apostolic times. The act of transmission should be performed in accordance with the apostolic tradition, which includes the invocation of the Spirit and the laying on of hands.

53. In order to achieve mutual recognition, different steps are required of different churches. For example:

> a) Churches which have preserved the episcopal succession are asked to recognize both the apostolic content of the ordained

ministry which exists in churches which have not maintained such succession and also the existence in these churches of a ministry of *episkopé* in various forms.

b) Churches without the episcopal succession, and living in faithful continuity with the apostolic faith and mission, have a ministry of Word and Sacrament, as is evident from the belief, practice, and life of those churches. These churches are asked to realize that the continuity with the Church of the apostles finds profound expression in the successive laying on of hands by bishops and that, though they may not lack the continuity of the apostolic tradition, this sign will strengthen and deepen that continuity. They may need to recover the sign of the episcopal succession.

from *Baptism, Eucharist and Ministry*, Faith and Order Paper 111. Geneva: World Council of Churches, 1982.

The Niagara Report (Excerpts)

53. What is essential to the life and mission of the Church is that the connection between the universal and the local should be made, and that it should be effective. The question which has to be addressed to our own churches is not merely whether they intend such a link, but how it is allowed to be effective. The mere presence of a bishop as what is said to be 'a focus of unity' will not *guarantee* the preservation of *koinonia* between local and universal; nor will the absence of such a bishop entail its destruction. The same is the case in relation to continuity. 'Apostolic succession in the episcopal office does not consist primarily in an unbroken chain of those ordaining to those ordained, but in a succession in the presiding ministry of a church, which stands in the continuity of apostolic faith and which is overseen by the bishop in order to keep it in the communion of the Catholic and Apostolic Church'. (LRCJC, *The Ministry in the Church*, 62) *

94.   Anglican Churches should make the necessary canonical revisions so that they can acknowledge and recognize the full authenticity of the existing ministries of Lutheran Churches. We believe that the basis for such action lies in the recognition that 'the apostolic succession in the episcopal office does not consist primarily in an unbroken chain of those ordaining to those ordained, but in a succession in the presiding ministry of a church, which stands in the continuity of apostolic faith'. (*The Ministry in the Church, 62*) Anglican Churches are here being asked for a major canonical revision in ordering their relationships to those Lutheran Churches which have bishops who are not in the historic episcopate and to those whose chief ministers exercising *episcope* are not called bishops. We believe that Anglicans are free to do this both by the grace and power of the Holy Spirit and because such action does not mean surrender of the gift of the historic episcopate. 'Full communion', the consequence of such acknowledgement and recognition, does not mean the organizational merger of Anglican and Lutheran Churches. Therefore Anglican Churches would continue to consecrate their own bishops and ordain their own clergy according to the ordinals now in use.

from *The Niagara Report: Report of the Anglican-Lutheran Consultation on Episcope, 1987*. London: ACC, 1988. (The Secretary General of the Anglican Consultative Council and the General Secretary of the Lutheran World Federation.)

* *The Ministry in the Church* is an agreed statement of the Lutheran-Roman Catholic Joint Commission. Geneva: LWF, 1982.

Together in Mission and Ministry: The Porvoo Common Statement (Excerpts)

IV. Episcopacy in the Service of the Apostolicity of the Church

34.   There is a long-standing problem about episcopal ministry and its relation to succession. At the time of the Reformation all our

churches ordained bishops (sometimes the term superintendent was used as a synonym for bishop) to the existing sees of the Catholic Church, indicating their intention to continue the life and ministry of the One, Holy, Catholic and Apostolic Church. In some of the territories the historic succession of bishops was maintained by episcopal ordination, whereas elsewhere on a few occasions bishops or superintendents were consecrated by priests following what was believed to be the precedent of the early Church.[37] One consequence of this was a lack of unity between the ministries of our churches and thus a hindrance to our common witness, service and mission. The interruption of the episcopal succession has, nevertheless, in these particular churches always been accompanied by the intention and by measures to secure the apostolic continuity of the Church as a Church of the gospel served by an episcopal ministry. The subsequent tradition of these churches demonstrates their faithfulness to the apostolicity of the Church. In the last one hundred years all our churches have felt a growing need to overcome this difficulty and to give common expression to their continuous participation in the life of the One, Holy, Catholic and Apostolic Church.

35. Because of this difficulty we now set out at greater length an understanding of the apostolicity of the whole Church and within that the apostolic ministry, succession in the episcopal office and the historic succession as a sign. All of these are interrelated.

A. The Apostolicity of the Whole Church

36. In the Creed, the Church confesses itself to be apostolic. The Church lives in continuity with the apostles and their proclamation. The same Lord who sent the apostles continues to be present in the Church. The Spirit keeps the Church in the apostolic tradition until the fulfillment of history in the Kingdom of God. Apostolic tradition in the Church means continuity in the permanent characteristics of the Church of the apostles: witness to the apostolic faith, proclamation and fresh interpretation of the Gospel, celebration of baptism and the eucharist, the transmission of ministerial responsibilities, communion in prayer, love, joy and suffering, service to the sick and needy, unity among the local churches and sharing the gifts which the Lord have given to each.[38]

37. The Church today is charged, as were the apostles, to proclaim the gospel to all nations, because the good news about Jesus Christ is the disclosure of God's eternal plan for the reconciliation of all things in his Son. The Church is called to faithfulness to the normative apostolic witness to the life, death, resurrection and exaltation of its Lord. The Church receives its mission and the power to fulfill this mission as a gift of the risen Christ. The Church is thus apostolic as a whole. 'Apostolicity means that the Church is sent by Jesus to be for the world, to participate in his mission and therefore in the mission of the One who sent Jesus, to participate in the mission of the Father and the Son through the dynamic of the Holy Spirit.'[39]

38. God the Holy Spirit pours out his gifts upon the whole Church (Eph. 4.11–13, 1 Cor. 12.4–11), and raises up men and women, both lay and ordained, to contribute to the nurture of the community. Thus the whole Church, and every member, participates in and contributes to the communication of the gospel, by their faithful expression and embodiment of the permanent characteristics of the Church of the apostles in a given time and place. Essential to its testimony are not merely its words, but the love of its members for one another, the quality of its service of those in need, its use of financial and other resources, the justice and effectiveness of its life and its means of discipline, its distribution and exercise of power, and its assemblies for worship. All these are means of communication which must be focused upon Christ, the true Word of God, and spring from life in the Holy Spirit.

39. Thus the primary manifestation of apostolic succession is to be found in the apostolic tradition of the Church as a whole. The succession is an expression of the permanence and, therefore, of the continuity of Christ's own mission in which the Church participates.[40]

40. Within the apostolicity of the whole Church is an apostolic succession of the ministry which serves and is a focus of the continuity of the Church in its life in Christ and its faithfulness to the words and acts of Jesus transmitted by the apostles.[41] The ordained ministry has a particular responsibility for witnessing to this tradition and for proclaiming it afresh with authority in every generation.[42]

B.   Apostolic Ministry

41. To nourish the Church, God has given the apostolic ministry, instituted by our Lord and transmitted through the apostles. The chief responsibility of the ordained ministry is to assemble and build up the body of Christ by proclaiming and teaching the Word of God, by celebrating the sacraments and by guiding the life of the community in its worship, its mission and its caring ministry.[43] The setting aside of a person to a lifelong ordained office by prayer, invocation of the Holy Spirit and the laying on of hands reminds the Church that it receives its mission from Christ himself and expresses the Church's firm intention to live in fidelity to and gratitude for that commission and gift. The different tasks of the one ministry find expression in its structuring. The threefold ministry of bishops, priests and deacons became the general pattern of ordained ministry in the early Church, though subsequently it underwent considerable change in its practical exercise and is still developing today.[44]

42. The diversity of God's gifts requires their co-ordination so that they enrich the whole Church and its unity. This diversity and the multiplicity of tasks involved in serving it calls for a ministry of co-ordination. This is the ministry of oversight, episcope, a caring for the life of a whole community, a pastoring of the pastors and a true feeding of Christ's flock, in accordance with Christ's command across the ages and in unity with Christians in other places. Episcope (oversight) is a requirement of the whole Church and its faithful exercise in the light of the gospel is of fundamental importance to its life.

43. Oversight of the Church and its mission is the particular responsibility of the bishop. The bishop's office is one of service and communication within the community of believers and, together with the whole community, to the world. Bishops preach the Word, preside at the sacraments, and administer discipline in such a way as to be representative pastoral ministers of oversight, continuity and unity in the Church. They have pastoral oversight of the area to which they are called. They serve the apostolicity, catholicity and unity of the Church's teaching, worship and sacramental life. They have responsibility for leadership in the Church's mission.[45] None of these tasks should be carried out in isolation from the whole Church.

44. The ministry of oversight is exercised personally, collegially and communally. It is personal because the presence of Christ among his people can most effectively be pointed to by the person ordained to proclaim the gospel and call the community to serve the Lord in unity of life and witness. It is collegial, first because the bishop gathers together those who are ordained to share in the tasks of ministry and to represent the concerns of the community; secondly, because through the collegiality of bishops the Christian community in local areas is related to the wider Church, and the universal Church to that community. It is communal, because the exercise of ordained ministry is rooted in the life of the community and requires the community's effective participation in the discovery of God's will and the guidance of the Spirit. In most of our churches today this takes synodical form. Bishops, together with other ministers and the whole community, are responsible for the orderly transfer of ministerial authority in the Church.[46]

45. The personal, collegial and communal dimensions of oversight find expression at the local, regional and universal levels of the Church's life.

C.   The Episcopal Office in the Service of the Apostolic Succession

46. The ultimate ground of the fidelity of the Church, in continuity with the apostles, is the promise of the Lord and the presence of the Holy Spirit at work in the whole Church. The continuity of the ministry of oversight is to be understood within the continuity of the apostolic life and mission of the whole Church. Apostolic succession in the episcopal office is a visible and personal way of focusing the apostolicity of the whole Church.

47. Continuity in apostolic succession is signified in the ordination or consecration of a bishop. In this act the people of God gather to affirm the choice of and pray for the chosen candidate. At the laying on of hands by the ordaining bishop and other representatives with prayer, the whole Church calls upon God in confidence of his promise to pour out the Holy Spirit on his covenant people (Is. 11.1-3, cf. Veni Creator Spiritus). The biblical act of laying on of hands is rich in

significance. It may mean (among other things) identification, commissioning or welcome. It is used in a variety of contexts: confirmation, reconciliation, healing and ordination. On the one hand, by the laying on of hands with prayer a gift of grace already given by God is recognized and confirmed; on the other hand it is perfected for service. The precise significance or intention of the laying on of hands as a sign is determined by the prayer or declaration which accompanies it. In the case of the episcopate, to ordain by prayer and the laying on of hands is to do what the apostles did, and the Church through the ages.

48. In the consecration of a bishop the sign is effective in four ways: first it bears witness to the Church's trust in God's faithfulness to his people and in the promised presence of Christ with his Church, through the power of the Holy Spirit, to the end of time; secondly, it expresses the Church's intention to be faithful to God's initiative and gift, by living in the continuity of the apostolic faith and tradition; thirdly, the participation of a group of bishops in the laying on of hands signifies their and their churches' acceptance of the new bishop and so of the catholicity of the churches:[47] fourthly, it transmits ministerial office and its authority in accordance with God's will and institution. Thus in the act of consecration a bishop receives the sign of divine approval and a permanent commission to lead his particular church in the common faith and apostolic life of all the churches.

49. The continuity signified in the consecration of a bishop to episcopal ministry cannot be divorced from the continuity of life and witness of the diocese to which he is called. In the particular circumstances of our churches, the continuity represented by the occupation of the historic sees is more than personal. The care to maintain a diocesan and parochial pattern of pastoral life and ministry reflects an intention of the churches to continue to exercise the apostolic ministry of Word and Sacrament of the universal Church.

D.   The Historic Episcopal Succession as Sign

50. The whole Church is a sign of the Kingdom of God;[48] the act of ordination is a sign of God's faithfulness to his Church, especially

in relation to the oversight of its mission. To ordain a bishop in historic succession (that is, in intended continuity from the apostles themselves) is also a sign.[49] In so doing the Church communicates its care for continuity in the whole of its life and mission, and reinforces its determination to manifest the permanent characteristics of the Church of the apostles. To make the meaning of the sign fully intelligible it is necessary to include in the service of ordination a public declaration of the faith of the Church and an exposition of the ministry to which the new bishop is called. In this way the sign of historic episcopal succession is placed clearly in its full context of the continuity of proclamation of the gospel of Christ and the mission of his Church.

51. The use of the sign of the historic episcopal succession does not by itself guarantee the fidelity of a church to every aspect of the apostolic faith, life and mission. There have been schisms in the history of churches using the sign of historic succession. Nor does the sign guarantee the personal faithfulness of the bishop. Nonetheless, the retention of the sign remains a permanent challenge to fidelity and to unity, a summons to witness to, and a commission to realize more fully, the permanent characteristics of the Church of the apostles.[50]

52. Faithfulness to the apostolic calling of the whole Church is carried by more than one means of continuity. Therefore a church which has preserved the sign of historic episcopal succession is free to acknowledge an authentic episcopal ministry in a church which has preserved continuity in the episcopal office by an occasional priestly/presbyteral ordination at the time of the Reformation. Similarly, a church which has preserved continuity through such a succession is free to enter a relationship of mutual participation in episcopal ordinations with a church which has retained the historical episcopal succession, and to embrace this sign, without denying its past apostolic continuity.[51]

53. The mutual acknowledgement of our churches and ministries is theologically prior to the use of the sign of the laying on of hands in the historic succession. Resumption of the use of the sign does not imply an adverse judgement on the ministries of those churches which

did not previously make use of the sign. it is rather a means of making more visible the unity and continuity of the Church at all times and in all places.

54. To the degree to which our ministries have been separated, all our churches have lacked something of that fullness which God desires for his people (Eph. 1.23 and 3.17–19). By moving together, and by being served by a reconciled and mutually recognized episcopal ministry, our churches will be both more faithful to their calling and also more conscious of their need for renewal. By the sharing of our life and ministries in closer visible unity, we shall be strengthened for the continuation of Christ's mission in the world.

E.   A New Stage

55. By the far-reaching character of our agreement recorded in the previous paragraphs it is apparent that we have reached a new stage in our journey together in faith. We have agreed on the nature and purpose of the Church (Chapter II), on its faith and doctrine (Chapter III), specifically on the apostolicity of the whole Church, on the apostolic ministry within it, and on the episcopal office in the service of the Church (Chapter IV).

56. On the basis of this agreement we believe
• that our churches should confidently acknowledge one another as churches and enter into a new relationship;
• that each church as a whole has maintained an authentic apostolic succession of witness and service (IV. A.);
• that each church has had transmitted to it an apostolic ministry of Word and Sacrament by prayer and the laying on of hands (IV. B.);
• that each church has maintained an orderly succession of episcopal ministry within the continuity of its pastoral life, focused in the consecrations of bishops and in the experience and witness of the historic sees (IV. C.).

57. In the light of all this we find that the time has come when all our churches can affirm together the value and use of the sign of the historic episcopal succession (IV. D.). This means that those churches in

which the sign has at some time not been used are free to recognize the value of the sign and should embrace it without denying their own apostolic continuity. This also means that those churches in which the sign has been used are free to recognize the reality of the episcopal office and should affirm the apostolic continuity of those churches in which the sign of episcopal succession has at some time not been used.

Notes

[37] For this, see the Introduction, the historical essays on *Episcopacy in our Churches* and J. Halliburton, "Orders and Ordination" in the *Essays on Church and Ministry in Northern Europe*, appended to this Common Statement in the full edition of the report (cf. footnote 1 above).
[38] BEM, Ministry, para. 34.
[39] Niagara, para. 21.
[40] BEM, Ministry, para. 35.
[41] Cf. BEM, Ministry, para. 34: commentary.
[42] BEM, Ministry, para. 35.
[43] BEM, Ministry, para. 13.
[44] Cf. BEM, Ministry, para. 22.
[45] BEM, Ministry, para. 29.
[46] Cf. BEM, Ministry, paras 26, 29.
[47] Cf. Niagara, para. 91.
[48] See paras 17–20 above.
[49] See paras 47–48 above.
[50] See para. 36 above.
[51] The historical background is set out in *Essays on Church and Ministry in Northern Europe* (cf. footnote 1 above).

from "The Porvoo Common Statement," included in *Together in Mission and Ministry*. London: Church House Publishing, 1993 (© David Tustin and Tore Furberg).

The Lambeth Quadrilateral

The Lambeth Conference is a gathering, approximately every 10 years, of Anglican bishops from around the world. The 1888 Lambeth Conference agreed on four items as the basis for discussions with other Christian bodies.

In 1893, the first General Synod of the Anglican Church of Canada adopted the resolution: "We desire hereby to make it known that we adopt and set forth as forming a basis for negotiation with any of the bodies of our separated Christian brethren, with a view to union, the following Articles agreed upon by the Lambeth Conference held in London in the year of our Lord one thousand eight hundred and eighty-eight, viz.:

1. The Holy Scriptures of the Old and New Testaments, as 'containing all things necessary to salvation,' and as being the rule and ultimate standard of faith.

2. The Apostles' Creed, as the Baptismal Symbol; and the Nicene Creed, as the sufficient statement of the Christian faith.

3. The two Sacraments ordained by Christ Himself — Baptism and the Supper of the Lord — ministered with unfailing use of Christ's Words of Institution, and of the Elements ordained by Him.

4. The Historic Episcopate, locally adapted in the methods of its administration to the varying needs of the nations and peoples called of God into the Unity of His Church.

Interim Sharing of the Eucharist

Text of the agreement as revised in 1995 by the General Synod of the Anglican Church of Canada and the National Convention of the Evangelical Lutheran Church in Canada

Both churches agreed to:

1. Welcome and rejoice in the substantial progress of the Canadian Lutheran-Anglican dialogue and of other national, regional and international Anglican-Lutheran conversations, and look forward to the day when full communion is established between the Lutheran and Anglican churches.

2. Recognize the Anglican Church of Canada/Evangelical Lutheran Church in Canada as a church in which the Gospel is preached and taught.

3. Extend until 2001, on the basis of the above, the relationship of Interim Sharing of the Eucharist entered into on October 1, 1989.

4. Encourage the development of a common Christian life and mission throughout both churches by such means as:

    a.   the welcoming by congregations of the respective churches of communicants from the other church and the encouragement of their own communicants to receive Holy Communion in churches of the other tradition, both where pastoral need arises and when ecumenical occasions make this appropriate,

    b.   the sponsoring of joint celebrations of the eucharist after consultation with the diocesan/synodical bishops concerned, using the eucharistic rite appropriate to the presiding minister (*Book of Common Prayer* or *Book of Alternative Services* for Anglicans and *Lutheran Book of Worship* for Lutherans) with an ordained minister of the other church assisting.

Evaluations of such joint celebrations of the Holy Communion should be shared with the bishops of the diocese/synod concerned, and with the ecumenical officers of the respective churches.

The presence of an ordained minister of each church at the altar in this way represents two churches expressing unity in faith and baptism as well as recognizing that there are remaining divisions which they are seeking to overcome. This implies neither rejection nor final recognition of the other church's eucharist or ministry

    c. the fostering of:

        i. regular prayer and intercession for the other church and its leadership,

        ii. local study groups in which the Holy Scriptures as well as the historical and theological traditions of each church are examined,

        iii. pastoral agreements which permit an ordained minister (priest or pastor) to serve the people of both churches, including presiding at the sacraments of the Church, wherever, and according to whichever rite, the local bishop of each church deems appropriate,

        iv. shared use of physical facilities

        v. common programs of education and outreach

        vi. reciprocal attendance at services of ordination and installation, although not yet participation in the laying on of hands,

        vii. theological exchanges by invitations to theologians of the other church to make presentations at conventions, conferences and retreats,

        viii. co-operation in areas of social ministry

Canadian Lutheran-Anglican Dialogue (CLAD I) Agreed Statements

April, 1986

The numbering of the paragraphs in these statements arises from their publication with the Report and Recommendations of CLAD I.

Agreed Statement on Justification

9. The doctrine of justification of sinners was the central issue in the Reformation of the sixteenth century. Since that time this doctrine has been interpreted in a variety of ways both within our churches and between them. Today, however, there is a far-reaching consensus developing in the interpretation of justification. This consensus is shared not only among the churches of the Reformation, but a common understanding of the broad thrust of this doctrine is shared with the Roman Catholic church as well. (ALERC 1982, pp. 8-9; LED II 1980, pp. 22-23; L-RC 1972, pp. 26-40; 1980, p 14; 1981, p 9.)

10. We can therefore affirm that our traditions understand God's justifying grace as follows: We are accounted righteous and made righteous before God solely by the grace of God through faith because of the merits of our Lord and Saviour Jesus Christ. This justification, although not in any way dependent upon good works, leads to good works. Authentic faith issues in love.

11. In our traditions the relationship between justification and sanctification has received different emphases. Anglican theology has not generally made a clear distinction between justification and sanctification, seeing them as interchangeable names for the same reality. Lutheran theology, on the other hand, although seeing sanctification and justification as linked, has usually made a clear distinction between these two. However, in both of our traditions, we understand sanctification in relation to justification not only as an expression of the continuity of justification, the daily forgiveness of sins and accept-

ance of God, but also as growth in faith and love both as individuals and as members of the Christian community.

Agreed Statement on the Eucharist

Anglicans and Lutherans both have high esteem for the sacramental life and liturgical worship; both have been strongly influenced by the liturgical movement in an ecumenical context. We, with many other Christians, rejoice in the convergence expressed in the World Council of Churches' statement, *Baptism, Eucharist and Ministry.* Anglican-Lutheran dialogues in Europe and the U.S.A. have discovered deeper procedures for sharing the eucharist. Similarly, our Canadian dialogue has found a remarkable identity in understanding of and reverence for the Sacrament. We recognize the centrality of the eucharist as one of the two great sacraments instituted by Jesus Christ. It is baptism by which people are made members of the Christian community; it is the eucharist which nourishes them spiritually and strengthens their unity with Christ and with each other.

12. We confess the salvation offered by God in the life, death and resurrection of Christ; we agree that the eucharist conveys the benefits of that salvation. In receiving Christ by this means we receive the forgiveness of sins, are reconciled to God and to each other, are nurtured in the communion of saints, empowered in love and service and are given hope in this foretaste of the feast to come. In receiving these benefits we are reminded of a broken and hungry world and challenged to a life of mission and service.

13. We are confident that we receive these benefits because while Christ is present in a variety of ways to the gathered community (in the Word of God read and proclaimed, in absolution, in the baptized community and the ministries exercised by its members) he is present in a special way in the eucharistic action. The presence has been described in various ways, but the reality which these descriptions attempt to express is that in the faith-full partaking of the broken bread and the sharing of the cup there is a life-giving encounter with our Saviour.

14. We are agreed that when we obey our Lord's command to "do this in remembrance" of him, that remembrance (*anamnesis*) is not a mere

recollection of a past event, but the making effective in the present of God's saving activity in the past. We understand this as not our own work but that of the Holy Spirit who is at work in the people of God. Both churches insist that only persons who are properly ordained and duly authorized may preside at the eucharist.

15. In the eucharistic action both churches believe the bread and wine, as Christ promised, are his body and blood. It is not our reception that makes Christ present but the Word and the Holy Spirit. Because we believe so strongly in the real presence of Christ neither the faith or faithlessness of the recipient, nor the worthiness or unworthiness of the officiating minister, can effect or negate that presence. Nevertheless the benefits of Christ's sacrifice are communicated to the believer only through faith.

16. In the context of this broad and essential agreement, a variety of emphases is possible: on various modalities of Christ's presence, on Christ's presence as the once-for-all sacrifice for us, on Christ's forgiveness of sins in the eucharist, on the role of the Holy Spirit, on the fellowship character of the meal, on the extension of the eucharistic action beyond the limits of the worship service (reservation, communion of the sick and shut-in), and on various means of disposal of the elements.

We are confident that because of the very substantial agreement we have discovered in this area, the eucharist is no obstacle to our drawing together in trust and love, but in fact is already an expression of the unity we share in Christ.

Agreed Statement on Apostolicity

As a community of faith the Christian Church consciously seeks to submit itself to Jesus Christ. This effort is reflected in the doctrine of apostolic succession.

18. Apostolicity means continuity in the permanent characteristics of the Church of the apostles. It is God's gift in Christ through the Holy Spirit. It is not confined to the historic episcopate but is a diverse reality which expresses itself in the teaching, mission and ministry of the whole Church.

19. *Apostolic Teaching* finds its normative expression in the Holy Scriptures. The Holy Spirit through such means as creeds, confessions, and councils has provided guides for the correct expounding of Holy Scripture. Chief among the creeds both Lutherans and Anglicans acknowledge the Apostles' Creed and the Nicene Creed.

20. At the time of the Reformation both Lutherans and Anglicans developed confessional documents which were seen as witnessing to the faith of the Church catholic by being expositions of the Holy Scriptures.

21. Significantly, both Anglicans and Lutherans possess a similar tradition of liturgical worship which points to a common understanding of the Church despite differences of emphasis.

22. *Apostolic Mission* is rooted in the sending of Christ, in the Holy Spirit, into the world by the Father and in the sending of the apostles by Jesus in the power of that same Spirit, a sending shared in various ways by all the members of the Body.

23. Within the Body of Christ the Holy Spirit confers a variety of ministries among which is a ministry of leadership bearing the authority of Christ over against the community and expressed in oversight (*episcope*) which involves fidelity to the apostolic faith, its proclamation and embodiment in church life today and its transmission to future generations. This special ministry of leadership becomes the focus and personal symbol of *Apostolic Ministry*.

Agreed Statement on Ordained Ministry

24. As joint heirs of the Reformation both Anglicans and Lutherans view the succession of ordained ministers as being within the continuity of the whole Church in the apostolic faith. As joint heirs of the catholic tradition both Lutherans and Anglicans share a basic understanding of the place of ordained ministry in the Church. Indeed, our studies suggest to us that the ministry in each communion exercises essential functions of the ministry that Jesus instituted in his Church and which we believe is realized in our respective churches.

25. Both Anglicans and Lutherans acknowledge ordained ministry to be a gift of God to the Church and thus of divine institution. We acknowledge that this gift is essential for the Church and is exercised in a public manner. As responsible to both God and the Church, it has its basis in the gift and commitment of ordination.

26. Ordination is an act of Christ in his Church. It is administered with the prayers of all the people and the laying-on-of-hands by other ministers, especially of those who occupy a ministry of oversight and unity in the Church.

27. For both our traditions *episcope*, which involves oversight, pastoral leadership and coordination is seen as fundamental to the life, unity and mission of the Church and hence is fundamental to ordained ministry. Both our traditions make provision for this oversight beyond the local congregation.

28. Our respective histories have caused Lutherans and Anglicans to value differently the office of the historic episcopate. Nevertheless, our mutual discussions have convinced us that these are not necessarily irreconcilable positions. Indeed, we believe that a sensitive reading of our two traditions on this matter reveals a significant convergence of substance couched in different theological terminology.

29. We therefore conclude that it is possible for Anglicans and Lutherans to acknowledge each other as churches where the Gospel is truly preached and taught and to acknowledge that the other possesses a ministry of Word and Sacrament that is fruitful in terms of faith and salvation for its members. We further believe that it is possible for Lutherans and Anglicans to affirm that the other possesses a ministry of Word and Sacrament which derives from the teaching of the apostles and the practice of the early Church.

30. Although such an acknowledgement does not yet permit a full integration of ministries, it would be a decisive step towards eliminating the scandal of our separation at the Lord's Supper.

Some Words and Terms

apostolicity that characteristic of the church that shows that it shares the faith of the apostles and continues the life of the same community that bore witness to to Christ's resurrection and received the gift of the Spirit at Pentecost

bishop: coadjutor an Anglican bishop elected as an assistant who will become the next diocesan bishop when the present bishop retires

bishop: diocesan an Anglican bishop who has jurisdiction for a whole diocese. There may be additional bishops with various titles: assistant, coadjutor, suffragan.

bishop: national a Lutheran bishop elected by the National Convention to preside over the ELCIC for a renewable term of four years

bishop: suffragan an Anglican bishop elected by a diocesan synod who serves as an assistant in a diocese, possibly with responsibility for a particular geographical area within the diocese

bishop: synod a Lutheran bishop elected by the synod convention to preside over that synod for a renewable term of four years

conference a Lutheran term for a geographical area within a synod, comprised of a group of congregations

convention a Lutheran term for a meeting of representatives of clergy and laity at the synodical or national level; each synod meets every two years; in the alternate year there is a National Convention with representation from every parish

deacon see diaconate

deanery an Anglican term for a geographical area within a diocese, comprised of a group of parishes

diaconal minister a Lutheran term for a person who exercises a ministry of service such as social outreach, education, music or administration; they are not, at present, ordained

diaconate for Anglicans, one of three orders of ministry. For much of Anglican history a person served as a deacon only for a brief time before being ordained a priest, but the order is being re-examined and renewed. In some places people are being ordained as "intentional" or "vocational" deacons, chosen from parishes to serve in particualr ministries of service in the world. Deacons are ordained and have a particular role in the liturgy.

diocese an Anglican term for a geographical area under the jurisdiction of a bishop. In Anglican polity, a diocese, and not the congregation, is considered the basic unit of the local church. Each diocese has a synod that meets periodically (some once a year, some every two years, some every three). The synod is composed of laity elected from every parish, (normally) all the clergy, and the bishop(s).

episcope the task of oversight, or supervision, which is exercised primarily by a bishop but which is also exercised by governing bodies and other appointed or elected persons

episcopate for Anglicans, one of three orders of ministry; for both, the state of being a bishop. Bishops of a church together are called "the episcopate."

historic episcopate the collectivity of bishops throughout the ages; in Anglican understanding it has referred to the continuity in succession in the office of the bishop

incumbent an Anglican term for someone licensed to be in charge of a parish; this is usually a priest

license an Anglican term for the permission that a lay or ordained person has from a bishop to exercise a particular ministry; "licensed clergy" are those recognized to be in good standing and filling a particular role within the church

metropolitan an Anglican term for an archbishop who presides over an ecclesiastical province (a group of dioceses). There are 4 metropolitans in Canada. He or she presides at a provincial synod and ordains the bishops in the province.

ordinal the liturgical texts and the "rubrics" (instructions) that accompany them, used for those being ordained as bishop, priest, or deacon. The ordinal has a particular place in the canon (church) law of the Anglican Church

ordinary the bishop who has jurisdiction in a diocese

pastor the usual Lutheran term for an ordained ministrer of Word and Sacrament; he or she is "rostered" and normally serves in a congregation or a particular ministry such as campus or institutional chaplaincy

presbyterate for Anglicans, one of three orders of ministry, to which priests are ordained; Lutherans consider pastors to be part of the presbyterate, although this would not be a usual way of speaking

priest the usual Anglican term for an ordained minister of Word or Sacrament. He or she is ordained for life but must be licensed to a particular ministry.

Primate the Anglican archbishop with a ministry of oversight for a province or national church; the Canadian primate presides at the General Synod and at the House of Bishops but does not exercise jurisdiction in a diocese

province a geographical area comprised of several dioceses; Canada is a province of the Anglican Communion but is in turn composed of four provinces, each of which is presided over by a metropolitan

rector technically an Anglican term for a priest in charge of a parish, or an incumbent, with particular rights

roster the Lutheran list of clergy in good standing

synod for Lutherans, a geographical area that includes a number of congregations, under the jurisdiction of a bishop.

For More Information

National Office Contacts

The Rev. Cindy Halmarson
Evangelical Lutheran Church in Canada
500 Portage Avenue, 4th Floor
Winnipeg, MB
R3C 3X1
(204)-786-6707 (o) (204) 783-7548 (fax)
e-mail: chalman@elcic.ca

The Rev. Canon Alyson Barnett-Cowan
Anglican Church of Canada
600 Jarvis Street
Toronto, ON
M4Y 2J6
(416) 924-9199 ext. 281 (o) (416) 924-0211 (fax)
e-mail: abarnettcowan@national.anglican.ca

Members of the Joint Working Group

Lutheran Members

The Rev. Alvin Miller (Co-Chair)
13124 Marine Drive, Surrey, BC, V6H 1E7

The Rev. William R. Bulger
240 Woodley Drive, Hinton, AB, T7V 2C5

Ms. Carol Christensen
168 Prince Albert Street, Ottawa, ON, K1K 1A1

The Reverend Dr. William Huras
Bishop—Eastern Synod, 340–50 Queen Street N.
Kitchener, ON, N2H 6P4

Ms. Annemarie MacIntosh
46 Picardy Place, Winnipeg, MB, R3G 0X7

The Rev. Dr. Roger Nostbakken
33-455 Pinehouse Drive, Saskatoon, SK, S7N 0X3

Anglican Members

The Ven. A.J. Cowan (Co-Chair)
Diocese of British Columbia
912 Vancouver Street, Victoria BC, V8V 3V7

The Rt. Rev. Fred Hiltz
Diocese of Nova Scotia
5732 College Street, Halifax, NS, B3H 1X3

The Rev. Mary Holmen
43 Farmingdale Blvd., Winnipeg, MB, R3P 2G1

Ms. Heather Labrie
904-6 Street SE, Slave Lake, AB, T0G 2A3

The Rev. Dr. Richard Leggett
Vancouver School of Theology
6000 Iona Drive, Vancouver, BC, V6T 1L4

The Rev. Iain Luke
P.O. Box 758, Humboldt, SK, S0K 2A0